CAMBRIDGE LIBRARY COLLECTION

Books of enduring scholarly value

Music

The systematic academic study of music gave rise to works of description, analysis and criticism, by composers and performers, philosophers and anthropologists, historians and teachers, and by a new kind of scholar - the musicologist. This series makes available a range of significant works encompassing all aspects of the developing discipline.

August Manns and the Saturday Concerts

Of German birth, Sir August Friedrich Manns (1825–1907) secured for himself a central place in nineteenth-century British musical life. Appointed by George Grove in 1855 to conduct the orchestra at the relocated Crystal Palace in Sydenham, he held the post for more than four decades, establishing a high reputation for the Saturday Concerts and attracting internationally recognised soloists. Manns was involved in every aspect, from developing the repertoire to taking rehearsals. Under his baton, many of the great works of Brahms, Schubert and Berlioz received their first British performances, alongside world premieres of pieces by British composers such as Sullivan and Macfarren. Secretary of the Guildhall School of Music, Henry Saxe Wyndham (1867–1940) published in 1909 this engaging portrait of a musician greatly esteemed by players and audiences alike.

Cambridge University Press has long been a pioneer in the reissuing of out-of-print titles from its own backlist, producing digital reprints of books that are still sought after by scholars and students but could not be reprinted economically using traditional technology. The Cambridge Library Collection extends this activity to a wider range of books which are still of importance to researchers and professionals, either for the source material they contain, or as landmarks in the history of their academic discipline.

Drawing from the world-renowned collections in the Cambridge University Library and other partner libraries, and guided by the advice of experts in each subject area, Cambridge University Press is using state-of-the-art scanning machines in its own Printing House to capture the content of each book selected for inclusion. The files are processed to give a consistently clear, crisp image, and the books finished to the high quality standard for which the Press is recognised around the world. The latest print-on-demand technology ensures that the books will remain available indefinitely, and that orders for single or multiple copies can quickly be supplied.

The Cambridge Library Collection brings back to life books of enduring scholarly value (including out-of-copyright works originally issued by other publishers) across a wide range of disciplines in the humanities and social sciences and in science and technology.

August Manns
and
the Saturday Concerts

A Memoir and a Retrospect

HENRY SAXE WYNDHAM

CAMBRIDGE
UNIVERSITY PRESS

CAMBRIDGE
UNIVERSITY PRESS

University Printing House, Cambridge, CB2 8BS, United Kingdom

Published in the United States of America by Cambridge University Press, New York

Cambridge University Press is part of the University of Cambridge.
It furthers the University's mission by disseminating knowledge in the pursuit of
education, learning and research at the highest international levels of excellence.

www.cambridge.org
Information on this title: www.cambridge.org/9781108068888

© in this compilation Cambridge University Press 2013

This edition first published 1909
This digitally printed version 2013

ISBN 978-1-108-06888-8 Paperback

AUGUST MANNS . .

AND THE SATURDAY CONCERTS

A MEMOIR AND A RETROSPECT

August Manns at the date of
his retirement in 1900.

AUGUST MANNS

AND THE SATURDAY CONCERTS:
A MEMOIR AND A RETROSPECT.

By H. SAXE WYNDHAM, *Author of "A Memoir of Sir Arthur Sullivan," "The Annals of Covent Garden Theatre," etc., etc.*

THE WALTER SCOTT PUBLISHING
CO., LTD., London and Felling-on-Tyne.
New York: 3 East Fourteenth Street. 1909.

Dedicated to

C. T. D. CREWS, Esq., J.P., D.L.,

AND THE

WORSHIPFUL COMPANY OF MUSICIANS,

WHO LIBERALLY ENCOURAGE BRITISH
MUSICAL ART.

Preface.

THE memoirs of August Manns can hardly be said to present the story of a romantic or exciting career. They contain no record of the hardship or obscurity that are said to be so often the forcing-ground wherein great genius eventually asserts itself. Save for a few brief months as a young man, he was hardly ever obliged to sit in enforced idleness in the whole of his long life; nor, except on the purely artistic side of his career, could he be described as a man of an ambitious temperament. True, for the art in which he strove so finely to excel no trouble was too great, no work, however hard, even a trouble. In and for that only was he ambitious. He certainly never strove to attain dignities and honours. They came to him—rather late in life perhaps, many of his grateful contemporaries thought—and he accepted them calmly and without emotion.

August Manns

His ambition and its fulfilment alike began and ended with his duty. That being accomplished to as near perfection as possible, he was entirely satisfied. And it is to be hoped that the record of such a life as this is not without its inspiration for those who come after.

It is, at any rate, in this hope that the writer has endeavoured to construct something like a readable account of August Manns' career. The materials existing were not extensive. His private life was not of the kind that obtrudes itself upon public notice. But little of his correspondence was kept, except some few congratulatory letters of later years. The record of his public life is told in the thousands of concert programmes that stand on many a music-lover's book-shelves.

The keynote of his character appears to be its absolute simplicity. As he was in public, so he was "behind the scenes." Intensely devoted to his family and his art, he sought the quiet relief afforded in his latter years by the one after the strenuous physical and mental exertions involved in the other.

Preface

The writer's grateful thanks are due to Dr. Shinn for much valuable assistance, and for permission to use the interesting extracts from his *Forty Seasons of the Saturday Concerts*. Mr. W. W. Hedgcock has also been ready and willing to respond to any calls upon his valuable time. The larger part of the book is compiled from papers most kindly placed at the writer's disposal by Lady Manns and by Mrs. Bönten, daughter of Sir August Manns, without whose assistance the work could hardly have been completed.

Other gentlemen to whom the writer is indebted are Mr. C. A. Barry, Mr. Oscar Beringer, Mr. Gordon Cleather, Mr. F. Corder, Dr. W. H. Cummings, Mr. F. G. Edwards, Sir Edward Elgar, Mr. Austin Fryers (whose interesting article in the *Crystal Palace Magazine* has been freely used), Mr. C. L. Graves, Mr. Arthur Grove, Sir Alexander Mackenzie, Sir Hubert Parry, Professor Prout, Sir C. Stanford, and Mr. R. H. Walthew, for permission to reproduce letters and other interesting matter. Thanks are also due to the Editors of *P.T.O.*, the *Musical Times*, the

August Manns

Windsor Magazine, and the *Crystal Palace Magazine*, for anecdotes of Manns which are included in the work. The author owes a special debt of gratitude to Dr. Hamilton Robinson, who, in spite of great pressure of work, most kindly undertook to read the proof-sheets.

For permission to print the extracts from Mr. Joseph Bennett's recently published work, the writer is greatly indebted to Mr. Bennett and Messrs. Methuen & Co.

It is perhaps scarcely necessary to say that it was not practicable to refer in any detail to the multitude of early programmes drawn up by Manns. It would be, without doubt, interesting and suggestive to print these side by side with those of later years, and examine them *in extenso*, but no such technical exercise is here attempted. It was not possible to refer to any but the " Saturday Concerts " and Festivals, and even to these, as the reader will find, only sparingly. Nor has any searching analysis been put forward of Manns' personal character and habits, believing, as the writer does, that the plethora of domestic detail beloved of the " Society

Preface

journalists " of to-day would be wholly out of place in the narration of such a career.

The task has been undertaken more as a means of permanently recording the myriad grateful voices of those whom Manns befriended to such excellent purpose, and for those many thousands unknown to him personally, yet to whom his figure and features were happily familiar, and to whom the story of his life must be of interest.

No extravagant eulogies are needed, nor exaggerated estimates of greatness formed by a plain record of the life of the son of a Pomeranian glass-blower, who alone and unaided rose to be the honoured friend of the greatest European musicians of his generation.

H. SAXE WYNDHAM.

December 1908.

Contents.

August Manns

CHAPTER III.

CHAPTER IV.

CHAPTER V.

Contents

CHAPTER VI.

CHAPTER VII.

CHAPTER VIII.

List of Illustrations.

AUGUST MANNS.

CHAPTER I.

Early life in Stolzenberg and Elbing—Enlists in army band at
Danzig—Becomes conductor of Kroll's Órchestra at Berlin—
Kroll's Winter Gardens destroyed by fire—Manns loses his first
wife—Becomes bandmaster of von Roon's regiment at Königs-
berg and Cologne—Resigns the army and comes to England—
Joins the Palace band under Schallehn—Dispute with Schallehn
—Is discharged from the band—Becomes violinist in an Edin-
burgh orchestra—Goes to Amsterdam—The *Musical World*
comments on the Schallehn episode—Manns reinstated at the
Palace as Musical Director—Letter of appointment from
George Grove.

It is a difficult task to measure and set forth
in cold print the oceans of enthusiasm that have
flowed round the head of August Friedrich
Manns. What associations does not the mere
recollection of that venerable and beloved face
bring with it! How many thunderous shouts
of welcome from the Titanic audiences at the
Crystal Palace, at Glasgow, Sheffield, Leeds,
and elsewhere have rung around the splendid
and dignified form of the great conductor.
What addresses of welcome, what banquets,

August Manns

what showers of speeches, what columns of
praise in the newspapers! The friendly carica-
tures alone would fill a small volume. And
through it all he remained unspoiled. He was
still the typically simple, kindly, humorous
Teutonic gentleman that some of us are happy
to think yet exists in great numbers across the
German Ocean.

Here was not merely a great personality,—and
that in itself counts enormously in a man's
career, for it means magic, it casts a spell
round the commonplaces of his existence, the
coat he wears, the stick he carries,—but even
more than all which is conveyed by the
indefinable mystery of personality, the name
of August Manns was nothing less than an
epitome of music in England for the last fifty
years. It is as good an instance of the occasional fitness of real affairs as you may chance
to find. It was right that a son of the foremost musical nation should come and teach us
the value of our own too often despised native
song-birds. It has become platitudinous to com-
plain of a lack of musical genius in England,
but for half a century or so August Manns set
himself the task of finding it, and how well he

Sir Michael Costa

succeeded is an oft-told tale. It is of the man who actually and literally "discovered" and tapped not only Arthur Sullivan's sparkling fount of melody, but to some extent those that flowed from the pens and brains of Villiers Stanford, Hubert Parry, Alexander Mackenzie, Frederic Cowen, Edward German, and a dozen others of whom mention shall be made later in this work, that we here set forth the life-story.

All are agreed that it is impossible to exaggerate the influence that the subject of this memoir had upon English music. According to musical experts, Sir Michael Costa was the first professional conductor—*i.e.*, one who devoted himself entirely to the art; but Costa's experience as a purely orchestral conductor was inferior to that gained in his operatic career.[1] The

[1] In a paper contributed by Sir George Grove to the *Pall Mall Gazette* in May 1884, entitled "The Secret of Sir Michael Costa's Success," he maintains that Costa's great plan was "Make yourself safe." Surround yourself with the best possible agents, the best assistants that you can obtain, quite regardless of expense, and success is certain. In the zenith of his career Sir Michael never moved without such men as Bowley to prepare the whole scheme of the transaction for him; Sainton, Blagrove Hill, Lucas, Howell Pratten, Lazarus, the Harpers, Chipp, and

August Manns

Musical Times of March 1st, 1898, says that in a period of eight years (1846-54) it only extended over seventy-three Philharmonic concerts and an occasional symphony at a provincial festival; whereas that of Manns covered a space of fifty years and heaven knows how many concerts. The spacious days of August Manns began far away in the time when Wagner was a boy of scarce thirteen years and *Lohengrin* was yet unthought of. When Manns was born in 1825, Beethoven had still two years to live; Schubert had still to write his greatest symphony (the immortal No. 9), his greatest and longest mass, his finest piece of chamber music, and an infinite number of noble works, including the pianoforte

others of equal eminence at the principal desks; Peck and Henry Wright to distribute the parts. With the perfect organization and efficient execution of such lieutenants failure was impossible; but the method was horribly expensive, and crippled the Sacred Harmonic. Costa was quite unable to train and develop second-rate materials—to educate an orchestra like Richter, Manns, or Rosa. His interpolations were "shameful"; his additions vulgar, unnecessary, and brutal; and his ignorance astounding. Grove very justly adds that in spite of all drawbacks we owe Costa a debt.—Graves' *Life of Sir George Grove*, pp. 124-125.

Celebrity in Embryo

sonata in G major, which is pronounced by Schumann to be its author's most perfect work. Mendelssohn had preceded Manns in the world but sixteen years, Schumann but fifteen; Meyerbeer was in the prime of his manhood. The production of *Oberon* at Covent Garden almost coincided with the second birthday of Manns, the death of its gifted composer occurring a few weeks later. If we may believe the biographer of Schumann, at the period of August Manns' childhood, about the year 1830, the general characteristic of music, even in Germany, was either superficiality or else vulgar mediocrity. Johannes Brahms was not born until 1833. Chopin, it is true, was living a comparatively secluded existence near Paris, but Gounod had not yet entered the Conservatoire. How impossible was it to foretell that in a little village in Pomerania these great gods of music would find their prophet, at that time a small urchin in daily attendance at the village school of Stolzenburg, near Stettin; but so it was, and happily we are enabled to give the history of those early years in the actual words of the

August Manns

great conductor himself, who retained a vivid recollection of his youthful days to the end of his long and strenuous life. The following account was found among his papers, and was, it is believed, written by him for one of the numerous accounts given of his career in the newspapers during the last few years. Here we have it word for word as it was written, and our only feeling of regret is the inevitable one that there is not more of it:—

"I was born on the 12th of March 1825, at Stolzenburg,[1] in Pomerania, Prussia, the fifth child of a family of ten, of which the tenth, my brother Otto, was born before I was thirteen years old. My father, a thoroughly good, God-fearing man, was foreman at the glass factory of that little village, earning about 20s. a week. He played the violin a little, and it was his playing which no doubt laid the foundation of love of music for me and my seven brothers. At the time when I, at the age of about nine years, began to take part

---

[1] Stolzenburg is a village near Stettin, a large town situate on the banks of the River Oder close to its outfall to the Baltic.

Aged Eleven Years

in our home music as a flautist, our home-band consisted already of two violins, a 'cello, and a horn. None of us knew the notes: we were all self-taught, and played dances, marches, and natural tunes with our own improved harmonies and orchestration.

"I, in accordance with the compulsory laws of education in Prussia, went to the village school after the completion of my sixth year. The teaching at these schools was at that time rather primitive, consisting chiefly of 'reading, writing, and arithmetic.' The school-hours were daily from 8 till 12 and from 1 till 4, and began always with the singing of a couple of chorales from figure-notation—that is, a system by which the notes of the major scale are indicated by 1, 2, 3, 4, 5, 6, 7, 8, a primitive sort of 'movable "Do"' of the tonic sol-fa notation.

"When about eleven years of age I had occasionally to take the place of my elder brother and assist my father in his work in the factory. He, dear good man, discovering one day that I lacked the necessary talent for a glass-blower, decided that I should be a musician. I was sent to the neighbouring village, Torgelow, where an uncle on

7

August Manns

my mother's side was schoolmaster, and where my
studies of the violin, clarinet, flute, and horn
began seriously under the guidance of the village
musician, 'Tramp,' a middle-aged man, who had
fought and been wounded in 1813 at the Battle
of Leipzig. He had received a French bullet in
his left hip, which the surgeons had failed to
extract, and which in course of the years from
1813 to 1837 had sunk down from the hip towards
the knee, wherefrom, after having caused the poor
man a great deal of pain, it dropped during one of
my violin essons to the floor, smashed to the size
of a thin two-shilling piece. Tramp was no
ordinary village-musician. He taught me the
violin and elementary matter of music from the
at that time celebrated violin instruction-book by
Rode, Kreutzer, and Baillot, a large book which I
in my youthful ambition copied stealthily almost
in its entirety. My progress as a pupil of Herr
Tramp seems to have been very marked, for after
about six months' studies under his guidance he
asked my uncle to permit me to join his little
village-band at the music he provided for weddings,
christenings, and village-inn dances, as a second
violin, saying that 'it would be good practice for

Apprenticed to Music

my bow arm.' Poor old fellow! his chief object was probably to pocket my share of the proceeds, an arrangement with which my uncle did not interfere. Thus, occupied with my musical studies and attendance at the Upper School (Torgelow is a large village, and has two schools), I reached the end of my fourteenth year; and after having been confirmed at the village church, joined my parents in their *new home* in the East of Prussia, a village called Gelguhnen, near Allenstein.

" The proprietors of the glass-factory at Gelguhnen were merchants at Elbing, a thrifty little town in West Prussia, and it was through the influence of these gentlemen, the masters of my father, that I became apprenticed there at the institution of the Stadt-Musikus (Town Musical-director), Urban; and it was their liberality which enabled me to obtain special lessons on the violin from Herr Franz **Gross**, a pupil of Ferdinand David, of the Conservatoire of Leipzig. These institutions (the Stadt-Musikus) were at that time, and indeed up to the gradual establishment of conservatoires of music, the musical nurseries of Germany. Poor parents apprenticed their boys to the Stadt-Musikus for three or four years as they apprenticed them to

August Manns

tailors, bootmakers, and other tradesmen. There were generally a dozen or so of young boys, who were taught the various orchestral instruments by the master and his elder pupils, and who had daily from two to three hours' practice in *ensemble*-playing. Easy symphonies by Haydn, Mozart, and some less-known old masters, were constantly practised, besides those orchestral works which were required for the concerts, balls, etc., for which this town-orchestra was utilized. This little band was also utilized for the theatrical performances of operas, burlesques, ballets, etc., etc. During my first season (1839-40), I had to play the second oboe part on the flute, and during the second season (no oboe-players being to be had) I was entrusted with the arduous task of playing the first oboe part on a C clarinet. At a subsequent season I was placed for principal viola, and lastly as one of the first violins at the operas which were produced in Elbing by the companies from Danzig and Königsberg. All in all I got on so hopefully that before the end of my apprenticeship I had secured a place as first violin in the string-band, and as first clarinet in the wind-band, and had even appeared at some smaller concerts as a solo-violinist and solo-flautist. I had

Conductor of Kroll's Orchestra

also been favoured by Herr Urban with special lessons in harmony and composition, and some dances and marches of my composition were sometimes played at the garden concerts and balls.

"Having thus come to the end of my nineteenth year, I, in order to escape conscription (military service being compulsory in Prussia), enlisted in the band of the 5th Infantry Regiment, stationed at Danzig, as a first clarinet, and obtained in connection with that position a place as one of the first violins in the orchestra of the Danzig Theatre. The Revolution of 1848 caused the change of garrison of this regiment from Danzig to Posen, where in the summer of 1849 Herr General Musik-director Wieprecht, of Berlin, found me and assisted me in obtaining an engagement as one of the first violins in Joseph Gungl's orchestra in Berlin, and subsequently introduced me as a solo-violinist at some concerts which he was at that time conducting at Kroll's Winter Gardens, with the result that I became from Christmas 1849 till early in 1851—that is, till Kroll's establishment was destroyed by fire—the conductor of Kroll's orchestra." [Many years afterwards, Manns recalled the fact that while he was at Kroll's in 1850, he met a little girl of about eleven

August Manns

summers who played the violin and who was named Wilma Neruda. He added, in speaking of the incident, "She stole my heart by the charms of her merry and sweet temperament as well as by her exquisite playing." It is hardly necessary to further identify the little violinist of 1850 with the great artist Norman-Neruda of the 'seventies and 'eighties, and the Lady Hallé of later years.]

"Having thus obtained a footing in Berlin through my success as a conductor, violinist, and composer of dance music, the road for a higher development as a musician lay open before me. I returned to my studies in harmony and composition, under Professor Hodvard Geyer (or Gyer), and benefited in every way by the high standard of musical surroundings which a German metropolis offers to an ambitious young musician. Unhappily, the destruction of Kroll's establishment [in February 1851] had also deprived me of my income. A couple of months without earnings reduced me once more to a state of poverty."[1] [Manns also suffered, at this time, the loss of his

---

[1] He told a friend, speaking of this the only period of his manhood when he felt the pinch of poverty, that he was reduced to pawning his watch to buy fuel, while his wife lay dying in great pain and in bitterly cold weather.

Wanted by Von Roon

first wife, a German lady, to whom he was deeply attached, and to whom he had hardly been married a year.] "A couple of months afterwards I received an offer of the bandmastership of Herr von Roon's regiment, stationed at that time at Königsberg, but transferred to Cologne towards the autumn. Herr von Roon (who is now immortalized as Count von Roon, the Minister of War of Prussia, who, in 1870-71 in conjunction with Bismarck and Moltke, *made Germany*), although not musical himself, had a very fair notion about what constituted good music. He wrote to his staff-officer in Berlin to the following effect:—'I can't stand my present bandmaster. I want a young man. Can you find out what has become of that young fellow with long hair who used to conduct at Kroll's before it was burned down?' I had to arrange several of Beethoven's symphonies and other classical orchestral compositions for his regimental band, amongst which was the overture to *Coriolan*, of which the transfer of the 'cello, viola, and second violin parts gave me particular trouble, because the clarinetists and bassoonists of the military band were unusually weak.

"However, I serenaded Frederick William IV with the arrangement at his visit to Cologne in 1852

13

August Manns

to his and Herr von Roon's satisfaction. [Not the least pleasant recollection Manns had of Cologne was that there he began a friendship with Joachim which was to endure for half a century.] Indeed, the three years which I spent in Cologne in the position of Herr von Roon's bandmaster belong to the happiest of my life. I had trained a string-band, with which I gave highly successful 'Concert[s] *à la* Strauss.' Herr von Roon, the officers of his regiment, and everybody else in merry Cologne, seemed to be pleased with everything I did in matters musical. Alas! the severe military discipline required of the regimental bandmaster was too antagonistic to the free and easy life of the popular young musician, who, moreover, was prompted by the not unusual conviction that he was destined for more elevated art. [In a newspaper interview, published in 1894, Manns spoke of the reasons which led to his retirement from the army as follows:— "Altogether I was eight years in the Prussian army, and formed a strong band. Life was pleasant, for I was popular in Königsberg and Cologne. Military discipline rather interfered with me, and when after a jovial evening with friends, I had to head the band of the regiment and play it out of town at 5

Under Schallehn

A.M. the next morning, a young officer, who was particularly favoured by the authorities, created an unpleasant feeling by looking too closely at the buttons of my coat; and once our youngster said the buttons on the tunics of my men were not bright enough. Such distasteful criticism from juniors led me to exchange the life of a soldier for that of a civilian."] I resigned my military bandmastership early in the spring of 1854. Just at that time, Herr Schallehn (who was also an army bandmaster), my predecessor at the Crystal Palace, came to Cologne, looked me up, and engaged me as his assistant-conductor at the remarkable salary of £3 per week, conditional on my playing E-flat clarinet in the band, conducting for him at rehearsals and performances as often as it pleased him, and to arrange and compose music for the extraordinarily organized first Crystal Palace band of 62 brass instruments, 1 piccolo, and 2 E-flat clarinets. I entered upon that engagement on the 1st May 1854, and, needless to say, did my very best to please my employer.

"All went smoothly until one day Herr Schallehn told me that a great fête would take place at the Crystal Palace in September [it was the

August Manns

28th of October 1854], in celebration of the
Anglo-Franco-Turkish Alliance, and that he wished
me to write a quadrille on national airs called
'The Alliance Quadrille.' He brought me three
big books of national airs, and pointed out some
which he wished me to utilize. I set to work at
once. The score was finished within a week,
and the parts for the couple of hundred of English
and French players were being copied by some of
the young musicians who lodged in the same
house. This done, Herr Schallehn asked me to
arrange this 'Alliance Quadrille' for pianoforte,
which I did, although very unwillingly, because
I do not play the piano. When the proof-sheets
of my arrangement were sent to me for correction
I found to my surprise this title :—

THE ROYAL ALLIANCE QUADRILLE,

COMPOSED ON

ENGLISH, FRENCH, AND TURKISH NATIONAL AIRS,

BY

HENRY SCHALLEHN.

I being told that Herr Schallehn had received £50
for the copyright of this arrangement, remonstrated
by pointing out that although I did not object to his

Unpleasant Episode

name appearing as its author, I felt myself entitled to the £50 which had been paid to him, considering that his salary amounted to about £600 per annum, while mine was only £3 per week. He simply replied that he considered himself to be the proprietor of all such work I had to do for the Crystal Palace Band, and that after my display of dissatisfaction with that condition my services were not any longer required, and the accountant had received instructions to pay me a full week's salary in advance and thus end my connection with the Crystal Palace for good.

" The [principal] musical paper of that time, the *Musical World*, contains the particulars of this unpleasant episode of my life in England. I had to submit to my fate ; began practising violin-playing again, appeared as soloist at some concerts in Leamington in the course of the autumn, and accepted subsequently an engagement as violinist at the beginning of 1855 in Edinburgh, in the orchestra of the German-Italian Opera, under the management of Mr. George Wood, as sub-leader of the first violins, by the side of the 'Scotch Paganini,' the father of Sir Alexander Mackenzie, whom at that time I used to see occasionally as a chubby little

August Manns

boy at the rehearsals near his father. During this
engagement, which began early in January and
terminated towards the end of April 1855, I received an offer for conducting orchestral concerts
in Amsterdam from May till October. Stopping in
London for a few days on my way from Scotland
to Holland, I received a letter from [Sir, then] Mr.
George Grove, the Secretary of the Crystal Palace
Company, in which he told me that the directors
had decided to make a change of conductor."

Here the reader must suffer the parting from
the vigorous prose of August Manns, which
naturally gains interest by the mere fact of
being in the first instead of the inevitable third
person, and must turn to the less forceful writing
of the present scribe, who will endeavour, however imperfectly, to continue the story so well
begun.

Some more attention may perhaps be devoted
to the "unpleasant episode," as its victim well
described it, connected with the first conductor
of the Crystal Palace Band.

Manns' description of the incident makes no
mention of the fact that his devotion to the

"Wonder of the World"

task of composing and scoring the work so
coolly annexed brought on an illness, nor of
the immense success of the great fête, the first,
or almost the first, of the wonderful series of
national rejoicings of which the great Crystal
Palace has been the scene. The building then
enjoyed, besides the glamour of novelty, which
alone ensured its success as a commercial enterprise, the almost continuous sunshine of royal
favour, as the permanent embodiment of the
noble dream of the Prince Consort. It had only
been opened a few months previously, on June
10th, 1854, by the Queen herself, with all the
impressive ceremonial of a great State function,
on which occasion Manns played in the band.
To turn from its glorious inception to the con-
templation of its latter days is indeed a heart-
breaking task. But for the present, at least, we
are concerned with the time when the Crystal
Palace was almost reckoned an eighth "wonder
of the world." Those who had visited the
Exhibition of 1851, the illustrious parent of how
innumerable an offspring, had departed whence
they came, unto the uttermost corners of the

August Manns

earth, spreading far and wide the story of the unique and extraordinary building, constructed of the two least similar substances it was possible to combine—one the embodiment of denseness, rigidity and strength, the other of fragility and transparency.

The high position of the Crystal Palace as a home of all the noblest arts rendered it imperative that the noblest of them all should be fittingly represented under its roof. The form that representation should take depended on the musical director. Herr Schallehn was the first choice of the board of directors for that onerous post,[1] and we have seen in what manner

---

[1] He was, it seems, recommended by a member of the royal family, who from their august head downwards took a lively interest in the Palace and its fortunes. It is curious, though, to learn on the authority of Grove, in a speech he once made to the Palace staff years afterwards, that only a few months before the opening the directors met, under the presidency of Mr. Laing, M.P., to discuss the future management, and it came to light that no arrangements had been made for the provision of entertainments. "Well," some one remarked, "we must have music," and thereupon Grove was asked if any applications

Crystal Palace Band

Schallehn interpreted the rights of his position as regards his sub-conductor. It was hardly to be supposed that the vigorous young musician would take such treatment "lying down," and the following extracts from the *Musical World* of November 18th, 1854, voice his natural and righteous indignation:—

THE CRYSTAL PALACE BAND.

To the Editor of the "Musical World."

Sydenham, *November 9th*, 1854.

Sir,—You being the worthy exponent of the wrongs of artists, may I trouble you to inform the musical world the treatment I have received at the hands of a person in "a little brief authority"? I am certain that I have only to appeal for justice to Englishmen—that which I am denied by a

---

had come in for the musical conductorship. He had received two—one from Herr Schallehn, the other from Herr Sommers, two Germans without position and quite unknown.

August Manns

countryman of my own—when I shall receive it, more especially from those who hate petty tyranny and counterfeitism, if I may so use the word, in that art which should be above anything mean or despicable. I was engaged last May to be sub-conductor of the band of the Crystal Palace. My duty was to play an E flat clarinet and conduct the band when the conductor was not present. I have done so, and, besides, corrected the mistakes in all the music played, the palpable inefficiency of the proper party not being able to discern whether the parts were right or not. I have tried also to put into some correct shape the collection of useless music, not suitable, nor ever will be, for the said band, purchased at the expense of the Company.

On the occasion of the fête in aid of the Patriotic Fund, I arranged a set of quadrilles suitable for the occasion, combining English, French, and Turkish melodies, together with some original matter added of my own, and christened them "The Alliance Quadrille." I had them well re-hearsed for the occasion, and they were played with *éclat*. I arranged them for the pianoforte, and gave them to Mr. Schallehn, the conductor,

"The Alliance Quadrille"

who said he could *sell them for me*. What was my surprise to perceive, in a day or two, my quadrille announced by a publisher in the City as "The Alliance Quadrille," *composed by Henry Schallehn!* I went to Mr. Schallehn and demanded his reason for so acting, when he coolly offered me one pound, stating that that even would pay me, and rudely informing me his name would sell them better than mine. I spurned his offer, when he stated for my impudence I should then and there be dismissed and leave the Crystal Palace Band. I have served in some of the first orchestras in Europe, and I have never heard of such uncalled-for and futile vengeance from a party in power. Whether the true artist could act so or not, I leave your readers to determine. I have made a full and true statement to the chairman of the directors of the whole circumstance, and it rests with them whether artists who join their band are to be thus treated for merely protesting against the appropriation of their property by their conductor.

I have the honour to remain, Mr. Editor,

Yours respectfully,

AUGUST MANNS.

August Manns

To the honour of the *Musical World* and its then editor, the eminent critic, James W. Davison, an instant response was made in the editorial columns to the appeal of the yet unknown and obscure foreign musician. It is satisfactory to think even now, fifty years later, that the confident claim of a stranger to the inherent justice of the English public received such an immediate and telling response from the powerful pen of its foremost musical critic:—

"An appeal is made to us in our columns to-day which we cannot resist. A German artist of the name of Manns was engaged by Herr Schallehn as sub-director of the Crystal Palace Band. Possessing the quality of a musician which the director himself so much needed, Herr Manns soon made himself very useful as composer and arranger for the orchestra. On the occasion of the performance for the benefit of the Patriotic Fund, at which 'Les Guides' and several military bands assisted, the sub-director composed a quadrille on national melodies at the request of his superior in office, Herr Schallehn. The director was so well pleased with the performance that he immediately published

J. W. Davison

the quadrille under his own name; and, according to Herr Manns, sold the copyright to a publisher for ten guineas. These unusual proceedings were protested against by the composer, but the only compensation which the director offered him in return was a pound for his time, which he said was ample compensation. However, Herr Manns did not feel disposed to give up so easily his reputation and profits to another, and continued his expostulations, which the director at last silenced emphatically by discharging the refractory composer from the orchestra.

"Thus, the poor musician is suddenly deprived of his means of subsistence, and for no other reason but that he is talented, and will not quietly allow another man to appropriate the fruits of his brains.

"The tale requires no comment; every Englishman will burn with indignation at such an act of injustice, and will watch with eagerness the result of the injured artist's appeal to the managers of the Crystal Palace Company. There is but one step to take, and we trust the directors will take that step. It is to restore Herr Manns to his place in the orchestra, and to discharge the man

August Manns

who, without talent and character, acts the part
of tyrant over the unfortunate men who are his
superiors in everything but salary."

For the moment, however, not even the burning indignation of public opinion could avail,
and thus Schallehn enjoyed his fleeting triumph.
He produced his contract, in which the iniquitous
clause conceding the product of his subordinate's
brains to him duly appeared; he claimed his
pound of flesh, and Manns had to go. It must
have been difficult, even for the sanguine and
steady young musician, to see where lay the
proverbial silver lining to the cloud which over-
shadowed him. The responsibility of finding
not only a living for himself, but the cost of
educating a younger brother, had to be met.
He recommenced violin practice, and from a
chance meeting with a friend who was about
to give a concert at Leamington, was able to
make a highly successful first appearance in the
Worcestershire town as a solo-violinist. For a
short time he was, it appears, able to make a
living there by teaching, previous to his migration

George Grove

to Edinburgh as a first violinist with Mr. George Wood. This occupied the winter of 1854-5, and kept him going until the spring, when he had engaged with a M. de Boer to go to Amsterdam and conduct the summer concerts at that place. But before he had left the service of the Crystal Palace Company he had managed to attract the attention of a gentleman whose word was law in the management of the great enterprise—viz., its all-powerful secretary, Mr. (afterwards Sir) George Grove. And here we must digress for a moment to consider the extraordinary, and we venture to think, truly great man who was to exercise such an extremely important influence over the subject of our memoir. In spite of the strenuous life he led, and in spite of the fascinating account of that life so ably written by Mr. Graves, it is curiously true that his name does not bear that pre-eminent position which it certainly deserves in the history of his time. To the man in the street he is almost unknown, yet none can doubt who study his career that he was one of the most remarkable men of his remarkable generation. He probably suffered by the very

August Manns

fact of his lines being cast among the "days of the giants." His marvellous versatility was, of course, all against his being remembered as the hero of any one great achievement. A man who was at once an able engineer, a self-taught but conspicuous Biblical scholar and geographer, the secretary to an enormous commercial enterprise, editor of a prominent magazine, and, later, the Director of a College of Music, and editor of a musical dictionary, and heaven knows what besides, can have been no ordinary man. This was the personage whose ear August Manns had evidently gained, and who "kept him warm with the directors during the Amsterdam period, and for many years afterwards." It is not necessary to say much more upon the painful episode of Schallehn's dismissal of Manns. The indignation felt by J. W. Davison was, one cannot doubt, echoed by the board of management, and by their great-hearted secretary. They probably felt that the action of the musical-director reflected no small amount of odium and discredit upon themselves, and so it came about that when Manns left for Amsterdam in the early summer

August Manns at about 29 years of age, 2 years before he was appointed to the Crystal Palace.

Valedictory

of 1855, he had the satisfaction to know that his complete reinstatement was only a matter of time.[1] He could not break his engagement with

[1] The only remaining relic of those far-away days to be found among his papers is the following set of valedictory verses:—

<table>
<tr><td>

TOONKUNST.

Lied
opgedragen aan
August Manns
op het Concert van
8 September 1855.
in den
FRANSCHEN TUIN.

</td><td>

THE ART OF MUSIC.

Song
dedicated to
August Manns
at the Concert
of 8 September 1855,
in the
FRANSCHEN TUIN.

</td></tr>
<tr><td>

U, Toonkunst, êelste kern van 't leven,

Die 't hart verheft, de ziel verblijdt,

Die zelfs aan smart iets zoets kan geven,

U zig mijn loflied toegewijd.

Uw taal is niet de taal der woorden.

Gij spreekt door oloeijender accoorden,

En war die taal in toonen vloeit
Door worden ziel en zin geboeid.

</td><td>

O sweet-toned music, noblest art of life,

That raises heart and soul to realms of bliss,

That gives relief to sad ones in the strife,

I seal to thee my lovesong with a kiss.

Thou speak'st not to us with the tongue of men,

But with a flowing harmony divine;

And when thy gentle tones are heard, 'tis then

God's voice that speaks in unison with thine.

</td></tr>
</table>

29

August Manns

the Amsterdam impresario without incurring a
heavy fine, and he wrote explaining his position
to Grove, who, in a letter dated from the Crystal
Palace, June 11th, 1855, replied as follows:—

DEAR SIR,

    I have laid your letter before the Directors.
They are anxious to have an interview with you on
the termination of your present engagement, which
I understand you to say will be on the 12 September.
At that time I think it very possible that they may
make an arrangement with you, provided that in the
meantime nothing should present itself to them as
more worthy of their attention.   Please let me know
if you are content to adopt this course.   I am very
glad to hear of your success.   If you write again, let
me know what your band consists of, and what
music you play.

Yours very truly,

Mr. A. MANNS.   G. GROVE.

    To this letter Manns' reply was evidently
satisfactory, for on the 21st July Grove wrote the
following letter, the original of which August
Manns kept carefully among his most valued
possessions:—

Recalled to Sydenham

CRYSTAL PALACE.

SYDENHAM.

DEAR SIR,

I should have replied to your letter of the 9th sooner, but that I had to consult my directors on the subject. I am happy to say that I am now able to offer you an engagement as conductor of the band at the Crystal Palace at the rate of £30 a month, from the day on which you begin your duties. In telling you this, I wish at the same time to say that it is desirable that it should be kept secret, at any rate for 3 or 4 weeks to come. In the meantime, as you know the Palace very well, you should be considering what number the band must consist of; also whether you would like to bring over any of your present players with you. It would be advisable not to make any promises to them till you have been here and learned for yourself what the performers now in our band can do. The number of our band is at present 58, but we should be very glad, if possible, to reduce it, as the expense is considered by many to be too great, and we should prefer to reduce it to 36, if that number would suit the Crystal Palace as well as the *Franschen Tuin.*

August Manns

If you should engage any of your present musicians, you must consider that after *7 in summer and 5 in winter their time is their own for other engagements*, and this should be taken into account in fixing their pay. You must remember that, as the conductor of the band, you will be bound to do all you can to make the music *economical* as well as *efficient*.

I am much obliged to you for sending the programmes; when you write again send me a few more. I like them very much, and would give a great deal to have such music done in the Crystal Palace. The overture op. 124 has only been done once in London in my recollection. Weber's "Clarinet Concerto," *never*. Berlioz's "Invitation à la Valse," *never*. Nor do I ever remember hearing of Mozart having written a finale to Gluck's *Iphigenia*. Your playing these rare works does you the highest honour. Let me hear from you as soon as you can, and believe me to be,

My dear Sir,

Yours very truly,

G. GROVE,

Mr. A. MANNS. *Secretary.*

Amsterdam Contract

There was some trifling hitch over the termination of his Amsterdam contract on the 12th September, as originally arranged, and he did not ultimately leave till a month later, but by the middle of October he was settled in harness.

CHAPTER II.

As we have seen, the Crystal Palace was opened in June 1854, and eighteen months later, in the autumn of 1855, August Manns was appointed conductor.

In a previous paragraph Manns writes of the then Crystal Palace Band's extraordinary construction of 62 brass instruments, one piccolo, and two E flat clarinets. He adds in a postscript to the MS. from which the brief autobiography reproduced in these pages is taken, that he should be glad if a little point could be made " in my favour by placing the difficulties of my work at the beginning of my conductor's

Established in England

duties at the Crystal Palace exhaustively before the public. Now, after musical art has had a home here for many years, both the people and the Press have forgotten that I found neither orchestra, library, concert-room, or musical audience in 1855; and that I had to battle with strongly-rooted prejudices against the so-called classical instrumental music, and that it was really a matter of patience, prudence, perseverance, and pluck on my part by which prejudice could be conquered and the road for high-class music could be opened."

It is, perhaps, needless to add that the appointment won the enthusiastic approval of the *Musical World*, as expressed by Davison:—

" The change will, we trust, lead to some necessary improvements in the band. Herr Manns has a capital opportunity of distinguishing himself. His resources are sufficient to constitute one of the finest bands in the kingdom, and we shall be glad to find the Crystal Palace orchestra achieve such a reputation under his conductorship. Herr Manns is too intelligent a musician not to appreciate the nature of his resources and the requirements of his public. It may be safely predicted that the music at the Crystal Palace will be one of its principal attractions within a short time after the instalment of the new director."

It must have been a matter of sincere gratification to the warm-hearted Mr. Davison to find how soon his wise and remarkable prediction was fulfilled. From the article by Grove himself in the *Dictionary of Music*, vol. ii. p. 207 (first edition), we quote the following account :—

" The music at the Crystal Palace was at that time in a very inchoate condition ; the band was still a wind band, and the open centre transept was the only place for its performances. Under the efforts of the new conductor things soon began to mend. He conducted a Saturday Concert in the ' Bohemian Glass Court' the week after his arrival.[1]

---

[1] At the very commencement Manns had to overcome prejudice in high places, for even Grove himself was of the opinion that a string band would not do for the Crystal Palace. He was converted from this view by the first series of Saturday Concerts (in 1855-56), for which a string orchestra was made up of the double-handed players of the wind band and about half a dozen extra strings from London (vide *Daily News*, 19th June, 1903).

Established in England

This is the programme [*see* Appendix (1)] :—

PART THE FIRST.

(*String Band in the Music Court.*)

1. Festival Overture .   .   .   .   *Leutner.*
2. Fantasia Brillant for Violin on airs from⎫
   Der Freischütz .   .   .   .⎭ *Moeser.*

   Violin, Mr. MANNS.

3. Solo   for   Pianoforte, 'The   Chimes   of⎫
   England'   .   .   .   .⎭ *Holmes.*

   Pianoforte, Mr. DARLINTON.

4. Romance for Violin, opus 50 in F   .   *Beethoven.*

   Violin, Mr. MANNS.

5. Overture, *Oberon*   .   .   .   .   *Weber.*

PART THE SECOND.

(*Wind Band in the Central Transept*).

1. Overture, 'Ruy Blas'   .   .   .   *Mendelssohn.*
2. Waltz, ' Des Wanderers Lebewohl'   .   *Strauss.*
3. Charivari   .   .   .   .   .   *Zulehner.*
4. Marian Redowa   .   .   .   .   *Manns.*
5. Overture, ' Le Roi d'Yvetot   .   .   *Adam.*

AUGUST MANNS,

Musical Director.

37

August Manns

"Through the enlightened liberality of the directors, the band was changed to a full orchestra, a better spot was found for the music, adjoining the Queen's Rooms (since burned), at the north-east end, and at length through the exertions of the late Mr. Robert Bowley, then general manager, the Concert-room was enclosed and roofed in, and the famous Saturday Concerts began."

All this, however, *bien entendu*, was not accomplished at once. From the programme of the first concert it is evident that the concerts were given, perforce, in different parts of the Palace. These were, in the Court of Musical Instruments (since known as the Bohemian Glass Court), in the transept, north nave, near the Fountains, in a temporary music-room outside the King's Rooms, and in an enclosure upon the garden side of the centre transept. The concert-room, or, as it was first called, the "New Music Room," was not begun to be used until the opening of the second season, on November 15th, 1856, and it was not until 1859, three years later, that it was completed.

Established in England

Another special feature of these concerts is alluded to by Sir George Grove in an auto-biographical speech he made in July 1880. This was the insertion of analytical notes upon the pieces to be performed in the programme for the day. It appears that, although the actual invention of analytical programmes dates back as far as 1840, when Thomson, the professor of music at Edinburgh University, started them, yet for their inception at the Crystal Palace, as for so many other good things, the audiences were indebted to Sir August Manns. These are Sir George Grove's own words, quoted on page 52 of Mr. Graves' *Life* :—

" Well, at the Crystal Palace, as I need hardly tell you, over and above my special duties as secretary, there was the music, to which I soon began to attach myself particularly. And here, again, the analytical programmes, of which Mr. Sullivan has spoken so much too kindly, originated entirely from the suggestion of a friend. We were going to celebrate the birthday of Mozart in 1856, when the Crystal Palace music was just beginning to struggle into existence, and Mr. Manns said to me how

much he wished that I would write a few words
about Mozart himself, and about the works to
be performed.   I tried it and that gave me the
initiation."[1]

For several years to come, however, the notes
on the programmes are occasionally signed
"A.M."—as late, in fact, as March 1868.   Later
in the same speech Grove paid an unstinted and
generous tribute of praise to the work of his old
friend in bringing the playing of the Crystal
Palace Orchestra to such perfection.   He said,
after modestly depreciating his own share of the
work :—

" But what is the use of possessing music, or of
analyzing it, unless it is played to perfection ?
No, ladies and gentlemen, the great glory of the
Crystal Palace music is the perfection in which it
is played. . . . And to what is this due ?   To the
devotion and enthusiasm, the steady, indefatigable

---

[1] Dr. Shinn published in 1896 his pamphlet entitled
" Forty Seasons of Saturday Concerts at the Crystal
Palace," and to this and other sources the writer is
indebted for much of the information that follows.   The
work itself is now scarce and out of print.

Established in England

labour of my friend, Mr. Manns. Probably no one but myself is in the position to know really how very hard he has worked and how much he has done behind the scenes to ensure the success of the performances that do him such infinite credit."

Upon December 1st, 1855, the Allegretto and Presto movements from Beethoven's Seventh Symphony heralded the performance at the Crystal Palace of some of the unique and immortal "Nine" which have so often been heard there. These were the first, second, and fourth, part of the 8th, with Mendelssohn's "Scotch" and Mozart's G Minor Symphonies.

On January 19th, 1856, the Orpheus Glee and Choral Union sang, and on the 26th January the Mozart Centenary Concert took place, to which Sir George Grove referred in his speech as the first at which an analytical programme appeared. At this concert the Allegro from the Piano Concerto in D minor was played by "Master" John Francis Barnett. This incident is thus referred to by Mr. Barnett in his interesting *Musical Reminiscences* recently pub-

August Manns

lished:—"It was one of the earliest of the Crystal Palace performances, before they had attained the grand proportions of the celebrated Saturday Concerts. I played the D minor Concerto of Mozart, and introduced a cadence of my own. . . . The concert-room in which I played exists no longer, for it was destroyed by the same fire which swept away that section of the Palace previously known as the 'Tropical Department.'"

On April 26th, 1856, a selection from *Tannhaüser* was performed, and of this historical occasion Manns, in the *Musical Times* of September 1st, 1906, gives an interesting account. He tells us that the MS. selection from which it was played was stealthily copied by him from a printed full-score of the opera brought by a young Polish count to Posen, in 1848, where the Prussian infantry regiment No. 5 (in the band of which Manns was first clarinet) had its garrison. These excerpts comprised the beginning, end, and some of the Venusberg music of the overture, Tannhaüser's pilgrimage, the festive tournament march, Wolfram's "Evening

Established in England

Star" song, and other selections which caught his fancy. Four years later, in 1852, Manns attended the autumn manœuvres with his regiment, and during his spare time arranged his sketches in the form of an opera selection, retaining as far as possible the composer's original orchestration.

He conducted the first performances from the actual scores copied during a space of three days and three nights, in which the printed full-score was lent to him. "It seems," he says, "that on the third night I had fallen asleep and that something must have gone wrong with my tallow candle, as my MS. had caught fire, and burned the right hand corner rather conspicuously. This damaged MS. was, to my great regret, destroyed in the fire at the Crystal Palace. My daily programmes from the very beginning included the overture and the battle hymn from *Rienzi*, arranged by myself for a military band, but, with the sole exception of the *Tannhaüser* selection, my early Wagner sympathies met with so little encouragement that works like *Die Meistersinger* Overture had to be avoided.

Manns, as we see, lost no time in bringing

August Manns

before the English public some of the "high-class music" of which he, almost alone at that time, had the artistic insight to perceive the value as a popular attraction. Heart and soul with him was, of course, Grove, and there can be little doubt that to their combined efforts was due the appearance of the D Minor Symphony of Schumann on the 15th March 1856. The great lights of the critical world of that day; including even Davison of the *Musical World*, who wrote for the *Times*, and Chorley of the *Athenæum*, were uncompromisingly hostile to the cause of Schumann, and, as Mr. Graves puts it, "it took all the missionary enthusiasm of Manns, Grove, and a few others to make headway against the coalition of Philistines and prejudiced experts."

In the February [1897] number of that invaluable repository of musical events, the *Musical Times*, there is an article by Mr. F. G. Edwards upon "Schubert's Music in England," which embodies an account written by Manns forty years afterwards of the first introduction of another great musical classic into England:—

Established in England

"Crystal Palace,

"*December* 1896.

"In regard to my first performance here of Schubert's grand Symphony in C in April 1856, I can safely report that at that early time of my career as conductor of the music very little attention was bestowed either by the manager or secretary of the Palace upon my doings beyond this: that I was frequently urged to avoid the works of unknown and unappreciated composers, amongst whom at that time were Schubert and Schumann.

"I had never heard Schubert's grand C major before I performed it here myself, but I was well acquainted with all that had been said and done for that marvellous work by Schumann and Mendelssohn. It was owing to the influence derived from those trustworthy sources that I purchased a full score and studied and performed the work. . . .

"I very vividly recollect that after the rehearsal I entered Mr. (now Sir) George Grove's office and stated in the most enthusiastic terms how deep an impression the symphony had made upon me, urging him to come and listen to its performance.

45

August Manns

He (Sir George) *admired* but at the same time
pitied my enthusiasm, because the work would
never receive the sympathy of a Crystal Palace
audience. However, Sir George did come and
listen to the performance, and it was from that
time that his enthusiasm for Franz Schubert's
genius took root, and gradually developed into
that active participation in the researches concerning Schubert's compositions which have borne such
splendid fruit and benefited musical art in England
and abroad to such a great extent. My performances of Schubert's nine symphonies in chronological order in the spring of 1881, together with
the many *first performances* of his works, have, I
feel sure, not been without influence upon Breitkopf
& Härtel's decision to publish their complete
edition, which now benefits concert-institutions,
musical students, and amateurs to such a highly
appreciative extent.

" I have reason to believe that my performance
of the C Major Symphony in 1856 was the first in
England, although I remember hearing one of the
members of my then very small band speak of a
rehearsal of it under the late Dr. Wylde, when,
at the close of the first movement, the principal

Established in England

horn called out to one of the first violins, 'Tom,
have you been able to discover a tune yet?' 'I
have *not,*' was Tom's reply. I quote these remarks
made by two of the foremost artistes in Costa's
band (then the only band in England) in order to
show how great was the prejudice at that time
against any compositions which did not come from
the sanctified Haydn, Mozart, Beethoven, and
Mendelssohn."

Mr. F. G. Edwards, in his article upon Manns
(1st March 1898), quotes the conductor's "fore-
words" in one of the programmes of 1856, in
which Manns points out that the compositions
of Beethoven, and even of Mozart, were "for
long after their first appearance received with
the same rapture and the same dislike by different
sections of the musical world."

However, in spite of all the work, zeal, and
discretion of Schumann's disciples, it was not
till some ten or twelve years later that they
began to reap converts to their cause among the
critics. In 1868 the *Pall Mall Gazette* published
a series of four articles, in one of which the
writer, said to be Davison himself, first showed

August Manns

signs of "hedging." But Chorley, as one writer puts it, "died impenitent," and made it a point to the end of his life to walk out of the concert-room at the beginning of the second movement of Schumann's quintett, to mark, it is said, his high disapproval of a certain chord in the eighth bar.

We must not omit mention of the music performed during the 1856-57 season, which included Beethoven's Eroica and Pastoral Symphonies, the overture to *Tannhaüser*, "The Wood Nymph" (Sterndale Bennett), and a MS. overture (Henry Leslie). During 1857-58 the familiar names of Charles, son of John Braham, and of Charles Santley first appear, and we notice the announcement in the programmes that "special trains run on Saturdays," an intimation that must have cheered the heart of the gallant conductor.

Mr. Santley, in his *Reminiscences* (Arnold, 1892), tells us that he owed his first engagement—which was for a series of three concerts—at the Crystal Palace to his success in singing in *The Creation* at St. Martin's Hall. He was then a

Molique

young man, fresh from Italy, and was glad to accept a fee of ten guineas for the three evenings:—

"The last took place on Christmas Day, 1857. Molique played two solos, and furnished me with an amusing example of pedantry. The orchestra played the overture to *Der Freischütz*. I happened to be conversing with Molique when it was about to begin, so I begged him to excuse me leaving him abruptly, as I wished to hear it; it was such beautiful music. 'It is very effective,' said he, 'but it is not music.' 'How do you mean it is not music? I always thought it was very fine.' 'No, no; listen, and you shall hear it is not music.' I listened and enjoyed it very much. When I returned to the artistes' room, Molique looked at me with a knowing twinkle in his eye and said, 'Well, you have heard?' 'Yes,' said I, 'and am delighted.' 'Ah, but that is not music. Did you not hear?' (humming the violin passage in the stretto). 'Yes,' I said; 'what about it?' 'It is wrong; the B must go to C, not back to G.' 'But,' I said, 'that would ruin the passage.' 'That may be, but I cannot allow it; it is not music.'

August Manns

"At the first concert of the three I was very much disappointed with myself. I sang the Count's air from *Nozze di Figaro*, 'Vedro menti io sospiro,' which did not rouse the audience to any enthusiasm, and by Chorley's desire the old English song, 'When forced from dear Hebe to go,' a dull song, quite out of place in a Crystal Palace Saturday programme. It had been scored, too, by somebody who had much better have left it alone. The small applause which followed my 'rendition' was bestowed out of compassion, I believe."

A name that was to become familiar at the Crystal Palace and famous among musicians generally, that of Oscar Beringer, first appears on the programme in 1857. As an infant prodigy, giving daily recitals and playing with the orchestra, he began an engagement "which lasted for the best part of nine years almost without a break."[1]

The next great musical event at the Crystal Palace with which August Manns was associated was the Handel Commemoration Festival in 1859. Previous to this, in 1857, the Sacred

[1] Vide *Fifty Years' Experience of Pianoforte-teaching*, by Oscar Beringer.

50

1858 at the Palace

Harmonic Society had organized at the Palace a preliminary and experimental festival under the conductorship of Michael Costa. From a copy of the prospectus of the 1859 Festival we learn that its promoters considered this first attempt was perfectly successful, in that it enabled the Society to ascertain the amount of duly qualified assistance, both from professors and from amateurs, which might be relied on for the Commemoration of 1859. It also served to test and establish the fitness of the centre transept of the Crystal Palace as the locality for the Commemoration. The only actual occurrence of Manns' name in the prospectus is in the mention of his band's performance, upon the intermediate days of the Festival, of selections from Handel's Italian operas and secular works. The conductor of the Festival and, very properly, the reaper of the honour and glory derived therefrom was the redoubtable Michael Costa, then at the zenith of his powers and fame.

During the year 1858 Manns had still further strengthened the ties that bound him to his

August Manns

adopted country by his marriage with Miss Sara Williams, his second wife, who, having borne him a daughter, predeceased him, dying in January 1893.

It must not be entirely forgotten, in recording the progress of music at the Crystal Palace, that the year 1858 saw the inauguration, by Arthur Chappell, of the Monday "Popular" Concerts. In these days St. James' Hall was newly built, and we must at least remember that it was as bold an experiment to throw open the musical Mecca of London for the "shilling public" to hear classical music as that of Manns and his board of directors to provide the same delectable fare for the patrons of the Crystal Palace. There were, however, besides these, the concerts of the historic Philharmonic Society, not to mention Jullien's Promenade Concerts at the Surrey Gardens and Lyceum Theatre. To these latter the earliest Crystal Palace Concerts were more nearly related than to the former, and the great achievement of Manns, of course, consists in the successful fight he made for the faith that was in him, that a

Early Days of the " Saturdays "

genuinely "popular" audience were as ready to
hear and appreciate great masterpieces of art
as to listen to those humbler efforts to "tickle
the ears of the groundlings" on which most
conductors of the day were willing to rely.

Mr. Bennett (*Forty Years of Music;* Methuen,
1908) says:—

" One must go back a long way thoroughly to
understand what a boon the Saturday Concerts
were to amateurs who hungered and thirsted after
better things than could be found in town.
Orchestral concerts in London through the winter
were like the proverbial visits of angels. . . .
This state of things sufficiently accounted for the
Saturday rushes to Sydenham, not only of cultivated
amateurs, but of professionals also. . . . All that
was great in the London musical world might have
been seen at Victoria Station on the winter
Saturdays as the special trains were backing to
the departure platforms. . . . It was not a company
of many opinions, but a band of worshippers,
having one faith and one soul. Before the concert
a gathering of critics might be seen at one of
the bars facing the music-room—those chiefly who

53

August Manns

cultivated J. W. Davison, and picked his brains
when they were fruitful, as mostly they were. . . .
'Tom' Mudie never failed these Saturday gather-
ings. He was a brother of the famous librarian,
and became one of the first pupils of the R.A.M.
Now and then, too, John Goss would pass our
corner of the bar and be summoned by Davison
to stop and join good company.

"The critics' gallery was that facing the
orchestra. . . . It was amusing to see how the
visitors in other galleries were 'all eyes' for our
demeanour, and with what interest they observed
the demonstration made in the seat of the critics."

By January in the year 1859 the weekly
Saturday Concerts had become an institution,
and it is interesting to glance through the truly
wonderful series of programmes arranged by
Manns in these early and tentative efforts to
raise the taste of his audiences. *En passant,* we
may remark that the Palace opened at 10 A.M.
in 1859, that the admission fee was 2s. 6d., and
that only for children under twelve did the now
universal shilling then bring admittance. The
string of performers engaged at the concerts

"Saturdays" an Institution

embraced literally every notable artiste of the last
sixty or seventy years. It is, of course, impossible to do more than briefly glance at the
greatest of them. Early in 1859 I find the names
of Arabella Goddard[1] (1836-); Anna Bishop
(1814-84), wife of the composer of "Home, Sweet
Home"; Madame Lemmens-Sherrington (1834-
1906); Catherine Hayes (1825-61); Madame
Rudersdorff (1822-82); Messrs. Montem Smith
(1828-91); Herr Pauer (1826-1905); Monsieur
Sainton (1813-90); and Wilbye Cooper, besides
many others of less repute. The music performed
during the winter season of 1858-59 included
Beethoven's No. 1, 2, 3, 6, and 7 symphonies,
seven of his overtures, three symphonies of
Mozart, three of Mendelssohn, three of Haydn,
No. 1 of Gounod, and an enormous list of
famous overtures, fantasias, pianoforte concertos,
marches, and miscellaneous vocal music, not to
mention seven entire works of a dramatic character: Beethoven's *Fidelio*, Costa's *The Dream*,
Glover's *Tam o' Shanter*, and Mendelssohn's *Son*

---

[1] Who was, by the way, wife of the famous critic, J. W.
Davison.

55

August Manns

and Stranger, Œdipus Colonnus, Antigone, and last, but not least, the *Midsummer Night's Dream*.

Mr. Oscar Beringer tells an anecdote of the aged Queen Marie Amélie, the wife of Louis Philippe, who used frequently to come to the Palace Concerts. He was, it will be remembered, still a boy at the time, but a boy of remarkable talent and full of dignified pride in his position of "solo pianist at the Crystal Palace." One day the old Queen sent him by her equerry a purse and a bag of sweets, and there was a severe struggle between the desire to keep the latter as a souvenir and the wish that they should fulfil their natural destiny. It is painful to relate that the grosser considerations vanquished the sentimental ones.

During the 1859-60 season, on Saturday, 2nd July 1859, the happy audience had the privilege of hearing Clara Novello and Sims Reeves (1818-1900), while the following week Henry Leslie's choir visited the Palace and sang works of Hatton, Thomas Morley, Arne, Smart, Pearsall, and Weber. During the month of July a series of grand opera concerts took place on

A " Spohr " Concert

Wednesdays, with all the great artistes of the Italian opera singing, but these were held under the baton of Signor Arditi (1822-1903) and others. On 20th August 1859, Mr. and Mrs. Sims Reeves gave a concert, and on this occasion the conductors' names printed on the programme were " Mr. Balfe " (1808-70) and " Mr. Manns "; and Sims Reeves sang " Sound an Alarm " and " Come into the Garden, Maud."

On October 1st, 1859, the artists included Mr. W. H. Cummings, while the following week Herr E. Silas made his first appearance at the Crystal Palace as a pianist, both of these gentlemen being happily still amongst us to-day, nearly fifty years later. The concert of Saturday, November 5th, was entirely devoted to the music of Ludwig Spohr (1774-1859), whose death had occurred on the previous 22nd October. Upon this occasion the programme contained a brief memoir of the dead composer that was probably from the pen of Manns, or Grove.

This evidently proved a popular feature, for a fortnight later, on the occasion of Schubert's Symphony in C being played, the opportunity

57

August Manns

was taken by Manns to print a charming little account of the composer that extended to a page and a half of the programme. He points out that the first performance of the Symphony in England had taken place at the Palace three years before, and "it is hoped that the Crystal Palace Band will not do less justice to it now than they did in their minority, three years ago."

In December 1859, Manns accepted his first engagement outside the Palace since his acceptance of the musical directorship. This was to conduct a series of promenade concerts at Drury Lane.

Early in 1861, on Saturday, April 13th, there is an indication of the policy, so consistently pursued by Manns during his career, of seeking the works of living composers and placing them before the public with all the consummate skill and capacity possessed by the finest band in England. On this occasion Balfe, Hatton (1809-86), Wallace (1814-65), Macfarren (1813-87), Sterndale Bennett (1816-75), and Henry Leslie (1822-96) were the composers so honoured.

August Manns at about
36 years of age.

Meets Meyerbeer

During the 1860-61 season Beethoven's Violin Concerto, played by Vieuxtemps, announced as "the great Belgian violinist," and Mendelssohn's Violin Concerto, played by Sainton, made their first appearance at the Crystal Palace. *En passant*, we may note that at this time the Crystal Palace Company's School of Music must have been an institution to be seriously reckoned with in the musical world. Among its professors, as advertised in the Saturday programmes, were Henry Leslie, who took a ladies' singing class and an evening choir; Manuel Garcia, who taught privately on Saturdays; and Julius Benedict, who gave pianoforte lessons; with Lindsay Sloper.

On November 9th, 1861, Ole Bull (1810-80) appeared at the Crystal Palace, playing a solo by Paganini.

On May 3rd, 1862, Charles Hallé (1819-95) and Stephen Heller (1815-88) both made their first Crystal Palace appearances, playing Mozart's Concerto in E♭ for two pianos.

It was of this year that Manns used to relate a story of his meeting Meyerbeer (1791-1864),

59

August Manns

whom he had not seen since the days when he was at Kroll's, in Berlin. On this occasion he called upon him at the Albemarle Hotel, London, to arrange for the performance of his Coronation March at the Palace. "Meyerbeer," said Mr. Manns, "sat down to the piano and played it through from the full score with an amount of spirit and refined rhythmic accentuation and expressive phrasing which fairly surprised me. I well remember how, when he started playing, a street band took up its position outside and started a selection from *Norma*, and Meyerbeer, quite upset at the interruption, hurriedly sent down a bribe to buy the silence of his rivals."

During his stay in England, Meyerbeer visited the Palace and came to hear a Symphony Concert. At its conclusion he expressed his admiration of Manns in the German fashion by throwing his arms round his neck and kissing him on both cheeks!

On March 29th, 1862, Joachim, then a young man of thirty-one, appeared for the first time at the Crystal Palace, and played Beethoven's Violin Concerto.

Sullivan's "Tempest" Music

On Saturday, April 5th, 1862, the music to Shakespeare's *Tempest* written by Sullivan, at that time a youth of 19 years of age, was produced at the Palace, and repeated on the 12th of the same month. It is well known that to this performance, which created a great sensation in musical circles, Arthur Sullivan ascribed much of the immediate success that attended his early efforts. He was still almost "in statu pupillari," having but just returned from his studies at Leipzig as first holder of the Mendelssohn scholarship. Yet so pronounced was the popular and critical approval, that the music was repeated on the following Saturday. Thus was laid the foundation of Sullivan's public career, in which Manns consistently encouraged and helped him as long as he needed assistance and encouragement. How warmly Sullivan appreciated this, the following letter written 33 years afterwards shows:—

GRAND HOTEL, PARIS,

12th April, 1895.

DEAR MANNS,

I was delighted to see that you were well again and back at your old post. Don't go and get

August Manns

ill again, for you can be ill spared. It was a real pleasure to me to be able to help you in such a small manner. I wish I could have done more to show my regard and affection for you. To-day is the 12th April: on the 12th April 1862 was performed the music to the *Tempest* for the second time. (The 5th April was the first performance.)

How much do I not owe to you, my dear old friend, for the helping hand you gave me to mount the first step of the ladder! I shall always think of you with gratitude and affection.

Ever yours sincerely,

ARTHUR SULLIVAN.

Among the interesting débuts of the following year was that of Miss Agnes Zimmerman, then a Queen's Scholar at the Royal Academy of Music.

But we had almost omitted to remark the entry of a yet more remarkable name in English concert programmes. On April 25th, 1863, the music of Johannes Brahms (1833-97) first became known through Mr. Manns' orchestra. The piece performed was his " Grosse Serenade " in D for small orchestra (op. 11), and the following are the

Madame Schumann at the Palace

concluding words of an interesting notice of the composer in the programme book:—

"This Serenade, though recently published, was written some years back, and exhibits perhaps less individuality than his later works, which are more independent of preceding composers. The movements are, however, very pleasing, and will favourably introduce this new composer to the Crystal Palace audience.—A.M."

In the early summer of 1863 Madame Schumann (1819-96) made her appearance at the Crystal Palace with great *éclat*. She, naturally, came much into contact with Manns, with whom she corresponded and formed a firm friendship. In a letter to Sir George Grove, dated June 4th, 1863 (see his *Life*, p. 96), she writes to express the pleasure she experienced in playing her husband's Concerto, "with your distinguished orchestra. Pray, say to Mr. Manns that the delight by the fine accompaniment let me forget quite at all the trouble and noise of the visitors walking outside the room. I shall be very glad to play again in one of your concerts next year."

August Manns

The practical outcome of the directors' keen appreciation of Manns' services was shown in January, when he received the following letter from them:—

January 15th, 1864.

My dear Sir,

I have the pleasure to inform you that the Board have resolved to increase your salary to £500 per annum, from and after the 1st January 1864, with the understanding that your Benefit Concert is not to be relinquished, but that any profit resulting therefrom is to be retained by the Company.

I am, my dear Sir,

Yours, etc.,

W. A. HART,

August Manns, Esq.,   *Accountant.*

Crystal Palace.

On March 5th, 1864, Schumann's well-known Pianoforte Concerto made its first appearance, with Mdlle. Marie Wieck (sister of the composer's wife) as soloist.

It is totally impossible to do aught else than glance in the briefest manner at the huge number

Success

of programmes, all possessing some special feature of interest, and many of them adorned by the names of artistes which were as household words from St. Petersburg to New York. These were the days of the giants, and if Manns' success was exceptional it was owing to the fact that the resources he had to draw upon were absolutely unparalleled for richness and extent. It would take an entire page of this work merely to string together the names of the pre-eminent artistes who passed in a continuous procession beside the conductor's chair of the Crystal Palace Orchestra in a single year. And if the artistes were great and innumerable, what of the incomparably brilliant and immortal master-pieces they were engaged in introducing to the British public? The period was one that can never recur, and it is probable that Manns must have many a time been almost embarrassed by the wealth and variety of the treasures that offered themselves for selection week after week.

At a concert on 19th March 1864, we find the March and Soldiers' Chorus from *Faust* performed, and this must have been, if not the first

August Manns

time, at least among the very early occasions on which the famous piece was heard in England at all.[1]

The programme on the 2nd April 1864 was of a more popular character, when Mr. (1830-79) and Mrs. Howard Paul's drawing-room entertainment, "Blue Beard; or, the Sensation Key," occupied the first half of the performance. On Saturday, April 16th, Manns' name as conductor was replaced by that of Signor Arditi, on the occasion of a grand reception and concert in honour of General Garibaldi, when Mario, Santley, and many other famous artistes took part. On 8th October 1864 we find a "brisk dance" from Sullivan's cantata of *Kenilworth*—written for the Birmingham Festival of 1864—performed at the Crystal Palace for the first time. During this year Mr. Santley's name appears more than once as a vocalist, and the first performance at the Palace of the intermezzo from Henry Smart's *Bride of Dunkerron* took place. The programme for the 5th November

[1] The opera had, however, been performed at Covent Garden in July 1863.

66

Press Support

is of more than ordinary interest. The soloists were Louisa (1832-1904) and Susan Pyne; and their accompanist, Mr. O. Beringer, a name still familiar at the Crystal Palace; and the programme included Mozart's A Major Symphony and Schumann's "Genoveva" Overture, the note prefixed to the former bearing the unmistakable stamp of Grove's writing, although the familiar initial is absent.

On the 12th November 1864, the entire cantata of *Kenilworth* was performed for the first time at the Palace, the soloists being Mr. W. H. Cummings, Mr. Santley, Miss Banks, and Miss E. Haywood.

On the 19th November, Schumann's No. 1 Symphony in B flat was performed, and the soloists included Mdlle. Sinico and Messrs. Ludwig Strauss and Wilbye Cooper, while the managers were now able to print discreetly enthusiastic comments by such papers as the *Times* and the *Athenæum* upon their programmes. The *Reader*, a paper now forgotten, actually spoke of the band as "worthy to be ranked for real effectiveness among the best in

August Manns

Europe, and the only band in England that takes a position analogous to that of the leading orchestras of Germany."

In the programme of the 3rd December 1864, Manns prefixes to Sterndale Bennett's overture, *Die Waldnymphe*, a generous and warm appreciation of the great English composer by Schumann himself, wherein he compares him to Spohr and Mendelssohn.

CHAPTER III.

By the year 1865 Manns' work at the Palace,
no less than his commanding personality and
lovable disposition, had endeared him to an
enormous section of the public; and the first
of those spontaneous expressions of the popular
esteem, of which he received several in his
lifetime, was shown in a testimonial organized in
the spring of the year. A list of the contributors
lies before me, evidently incomplete, but of
sufficient completeness to afford some idea of
the widespread popularity of its object. The
amounts contributed range from 2s. 6d. to £10;
there are between 300 and 400 subscribers, and
among them it is pleasant to find the name of
Michael Costa, as well as those of Manns' brother-
officials—George Grove, Scott Russell, R. K.

69

August Manns

Bowley, and of many famous musicians of the day—W. H. Cummings, Frederick Clay (1838-89; composer of "I'll sing thee Songs of Araby" and "She wandered down the Mountain-side"), Henry Chorley (the *Times* critic), W. H. Cusins (1833-93), Madame Rudersdorff, Madame Parepa (1836-74), Arthur Sullivan (a generous contributor, although his finances were at this time none too flourishing), Otto Goldschmidt (1829-1907), Charles Hallé, Madame Lemmens-Sherrington, and many others of less note. A sum of £200, together with a clock and a pair of vases, were presented to Mr. Manns by Mr. Scott Russell, the manager of the Palace at the time, on behalf of the subscribers, and form an early evidence of the affection already felt for Manns by the Crystal Palace habitués.

A note to the programme for October 7th, 1865, informs the public that "by next Saturday the Concert-room will be entirely enclosed, additional space being added thereto on the south side." In November 1865, the Crystal Palace Choir first performed Beethoven's "Choral Fantasia," Madame Arabella Goddard being at the piano.

Handel

On the 21st October, Manns gave the public a foretaste of his powers in dealing with Handel's music, when for the first time at the Saturday concerts *Acis and Galatea* was performed, the soloists including Montem Smith and Weiss (1820-67).

It will perhaps lighten the readers' way over a possibly somewhat monotonous record of concerts innumerable if extracts are occasionally given from the remarks, always forcible and well expressed, which Manns himself contributed to these early programmes. On the occasion of the second *Acis and Galatea* performance he prefaces the little discourse with a brief synopsis of the old legend, of the circumstances under which Handel used Gay's libretto, and of the method of the early performances. He shows how the famous additional accompaniments by Mozart came to be needed, and remarks upon the reticence and modesty with which Mozart accomplished his task:—

" In what he forbore to do, no less than in what he did, he has left a model to be followed by all musicians. This is due partly to the date of his

August Manns

birth and partly to the modesty and simple refinement of his nature. It has been beautifully said—

> 'Two worlds at once they view
> Who stand upon the confines of the new,'

and in the world of art this is truer of Mozart than of any other composer. He more than any one stood on the confines of the two worlds of music. He was trained by masters who were the contemporaries of Handel and of the old school, while he was himself the great creator and master of the new. But striking as was his genius, it was not more striking than his respect and piety towards his great predecessor's qualities, which manifest themselves in every line of his letters and in every bar of his accompaniments to *Acis and Galatea.*—A.M.''

The following week Miss Emily Soldene—in whose memoirs so many racy stories are well told—sang, with Signor Li Calsi and Signor Foli (1837-99). At the concert on December 9th, 1865, Manns' foreword to Schumann's Symphony No. 2 in C major extended to two pages of the programme, in honour of its first performance under his baton. He begins :—

Schumann

"It gives me heartfelt gratification to introduce another of Schumann's great orchestral compositions to an audience which has so often ratified my efforts to make them acquainted with works more or less unknown. The two of his symphonies which are already included in the Crystal Palace repertoire have become established favourites, as I was sure they would do. . . . I venture to-day to add a third . . . and, further, to predict for it sooner or later a success equal to that of the others."

He then relates the history of the masterpiece in some detail, mentioning the fact of its having only once before been performed in England, at the Philharmonic Society in the previous season. He ascribes this seeming neglect of the great composer to the fact that "his genius often carried him into regions with which the taste of the musical public is not yet familiar. In the first twenty or thirty of his works (mostly for pianoforte) he attempted to illustrate characteristics and events closely connected with himself; and in this endeavour to discover a musical language for his emotions he not unnaturally invaded the cherished traditions of the

73

August Manns

musical art, and thus inevitably obscured those channels through which alone music can be pleasantly and intelligibly conveyed to the human heart. But, prejudicial as this proved to Schumann's immediate success, the art of music became a great gainer by his thus unrestrainedly following up the development of his individuality with the perseverance natural to true genius."

In the recently-published *Life of Sterndale Bennett,* by his son, we are told that "Bennett's retirement from the [Philharmonic] concert-room coincided closely, in point of time, with the general acceptance by this country of the music of Robert Schumann." While by no means in agreement with those who hold that Bennett "felt little or no love for Schumann's music,"[1]

---

[1] Mr. B. W. Findon, in his recently published work, *Sir Arthur Sullivan and his Operas,* quotes Sullivan's account of Bennett's view of Schumann as follows :—" He (Bennett) was, however, bitterly prejudiced against the new school, as he called it. He would not have a note of Schumann ; and as for Wagner, he was outside the pale of criticism."

Sterndale Bennett

his biographer recognizes and explains the fact that such admiration as he felt was strictly temperate and not, perhaps, enthusiastic. It is perhaps permissible to comment also on the omission from this admirable and lengthy account of Bennett's life of any reference to the work carried on by Manns. There are, it is true, two pages on which his name is just mentioned, but it is at least curious that it did not occur to the biographer—who claims for his subject a knowledge of and feeling for the music with which he had to deal, of an order higher than could be claimed for other conductors who were doing similar work elsewhere in London—that from the 15th March 1856, when *The Naiads* was first heard at the Palace, there was seldom a season that passed without at least one admirable and sympathetic rendering of a composition by Sterndale Bennett.

Manns' untiring efforts to popularize the music of Schumann were continued in February 1866, and his introductory note to the programme of the 3rd February (when the No. 1 Symphony in B flat was played) reminded the audience of

75

August Manns

the persistent opposition met with at one time by Beethoven himself, whose music, when played by Spohr about 1806, was dismissed as mere grotesque trash by those foremost in the musical profession of the day. Mozart's similar experience is well known; and Mendelssohn, "even on account of that fairy music now prized as one of his most characteristic and delightful achievements, was not suffered to remain without attack."

The concert of March 10th, 1866, is interesting, for on that date Manns introduced to the public a young German violin-player twenty-three years of age, who figured in the programme as Herr Carl Rose. The other soloists were Madame Parepa, whom the violinist married four years later (when he altered his name to its more widely-known form of Rosa), and Mr. Santley.

On April 14th, 1866, the performance of Beethoven's "Choral Symphony,"[1] although it

---

[1] On this occasion the artistes were Madame Parepa, Miss Julia Elton, Mr. W. H. Cummings, and Mr. Lewis Thomas (1826-96).

Schubert

had been done three times since its first performance the previous spring, evoked a long and sympathetic note from Manns in the programme. He vividly describes its various movements and their effect upon the audiences before whom he had conducted the performances; and the earnest, reverent description of the semi-sacred theme ends thus:—

"The big heart which forty-four years ago poured forth these mighty strains has long since ceased to beat, but thousands have bowed and millions will yet bow before its never-dying greatness. That the Crystal Palace audience of this day may be among that number, and thus by their approval cheer and reward all those who have striven to set before them in its true greatness this immortal work, is my earnest and humble hope.—A. MANNS."

In April 1866 there was another performance of Schubert's Symphony in C, described by Manns in the programme as "one of the most imaginative, romantic, and therefore interesting works in the whole range of modern music."

August Manns

It is impossible to overlook the advertisements of interesting events, other than musical, which occur in the turning over of these early programmes. Among them at this time was the announcement of "Mr. Charles Dickens' Reading of the Story of Little Dombey." The name of James Coward, the famous organist, and father of the scarcely less celebrated artiste of Mustel-organ fame, is continually met with; as is that of John Maddison Morton, the author of *Box and Cox*, who gave humorous readings in the "Lecture Theatre of the Tropical Department." Later in the season the Christmas pantomime of *Little Miss Muffit* is advertised, and in this connection it may be recalled to the memory of many faithful friends of the great conductor, that his wide experience ranged, as the steam-hammer does, from the "forging" of a great Beethoven performance to "cracking the nut" of the music to a pantomime. Many who are still living can doubtless recollect the genial musician directing his band accompaniment to the evolutions of the ballet-dancers as energetically and wholeheartedly as he devoted himself to the immortal

August Manns at
43 years of age.

Schubert's "Rosamunde"

works of the great masters. Be it said, however, that in thus performing faithfully his share of the bargain with his employers, he always felt he was being given "journeyman's work," which might and should have been entrusted to a capable musician of inferior calibre, without in any way damaging the prestige either of the pantomime or the Crystal Palace directors.

At the beginning of the 1866-67 season, Herr Wilhelmj (1845-1908), the violinist, made his first appearance at the Palace. A little later, Schumann's Symphony No. 2, which had only been played for the first time about the middle of the previous season, was repeated by request.

At the same concert, Mme. Arabella Goddard played Sterndale Bennett's Concerto in C minor. On November 10th, the "Incidental Music to the *Drama of Rosamunde*," which has since achieved such enormous popularity, was heard for the first time in England, and at once created an extraordinary impression among the critics present. The story of the discovery of its missing parts by Grove and Sullivan during their famous journey to Vienna in the autumn of 1868, is too well

August Manns

known to musicians to need repetition here. Those interested in the matter can read the vivid account by Grove himself, in his *Life* by Mr. C. L. Graves. The following remarks by Manns in the programme are well worth reprinting:—

"The compositions which are to-day for the first time presented to an English audience, form the principal portion of the incidental music written by Schubert to the *Drama of Rosamunde*, by Madame Helmina Chezy, a literary German lady, whose only claim to recollection is derived from her connection with Schubert in the drama before us. . . . Madame Chezy's heroine was not the Rosamond with whom we are familiar, . . . but . . . a mere figment of Madame Chezy's invention. Her drama . . . appears to be . . . in fact, a tremendous tragedy. It was written for the Vienna Theatre in 1823, but only survived two representations."

To this introductory note there follows a full list of the 7 numbers of which the music consists, and an explanation that the overture usually known by the name of " Rosamunde," was written by Schubert for the " Zauberharfe " or " Magic

" Alfonso and Estrella "

Harp," and that the overture actually played at the performance in Vienna was that of *Alfonso and Estrella*. Owing to a difficulty in getting some of the orchestral parts, Manns was obliged to confine the performance to the two Entr'actes and the Romance, sung by Madame Enequist, of which he says:—

" The two instrumental pieces differ widely in character. The first (in B minor) is a movement of some length, not in any regular musical form, but very dramatic and passionate in character. The two principal themes are of great beauty and pathos, and they are treated in so varied a manner, with modulations so unexpected and so touching, that the effect is most admirable. The second in B-flat is an air (Andantino), the commencement of which recalls Schubert's favourite ' Impromptu,' in the same key— with two Trios. This, though wanting in the variety and impetuous force of the other, is full of tender grace and feeling, and characteristic of its author in every note. It is impossible to say anything satisfactory on the relation of the Entr'actes to the Tragedy itself, unless we knew where they are placed—which we do not. The Romance, like so

many of Schubert's finest songs, is simplicity itself,
a simplicity the sweet grace of which has something
infinitely attractive about it.—A.M."

Manns modestly omits mention of the fact that
the accompaniment for the orchestra was scored
by himself, as the *Times* critic puts it, "with good
taste and extreme ability."

In the same month Manns carried still farther
his qualifications for the strenuous task of a
festival conductor by a performance of *Alexander's
Feast.*

At this time (November 12th, 1866), the
directors of the Palace had been urged to afford
their conductor some increase in the numerical
strength of his orchestra, and this they now
complied with, the band totalling 30 violins, 10
violas, and 16 violoncellos and basses, besides the
wind instruments.

In the *Rosamunde* concert, Manns remarks upon
the overture to *Genoveva:*—

"This overture, to the only opera which
Schumann ever attempted, was composed in the
year 1847, and stands as opus 81 in the catalogue of

"Genoveva" Overture

his works. It is not built upon the themes of the opera, but appears to be an attempt to portray the general spirit of the story, more after the model of Beethoven's overtures to *Egmont* and *Fidelio*."

Space forbids our quotation of the admirable summary of the plot, in itself a commonplace one enough, but the following remarks upon the spirit of the music by its interpreter are quite characteristic of the keen interest he felt in his work :—

"In what measure this story of passion and distress is reflected in Schumann's music every hearer will judge for himself. To us the sombre Introduction, with its sharp dissonances and plaintive violin figure, well expresses the inconsolable grief of Genoveva in her lonely banishment; while the Allegro, in the restless unhappiness of its principal subject—the cheerful melody given out by the horns, and repeated in the flutes, oboes, and clarinets—the charming second subject, the sudden and striking changes of key, and the exulting joy of the conclusion, reflects forcibly the anguish of the innocent sufferer, her occasional gleams of hope and her final triumphant return to her former

August Manns

happiness. The whole overture abounds with fine points and is a truly original and characteristic work."

It is perhaps not directly concerned with our subject, but some reference must be made to the well-nigh irreparable misfortune that befel the fairy Palace at which so much that was good and ennobling in art, amusement, and industry was being and had been accomplished.

On the afternoon of Sunday, 30th December 1866, a great part of the supposedly fire-proof structure caught fire and was totally destroyed. The fire originated, it was said, from the over-heating of a boiler under the Tropical Department at the north end of the Palace, which was cut off from the rest of the building by a great wooden screen. Immediately above the boiler was the huge Californian tree trunk, over 100 feet high, and this being as dry as tinder, gave the flames a tremendous hold. By one of those fatalities before which one is dumb, the fire burst out at a time when the enormous building was totally empty, save for a solitary watchman, a policeman, and an attendant upon the aviary and

Fire at Crystal Palace

monkey-house. At 1.20 all was apparently safe and sound; before 2 P.M., half an hour later, it was a burning fiery furnace. Some passers-by who tried to get in were unable to do so for nearly an hour. When they did, all hope of saving that end of the building was seen to be lost. However, they acted vigorously, and calling some loitering navvies in from the road outside, they tore up the flooring, and sent messengers in every direction for help. By 4.30 o'clock, Captain Shaw arrived with a force of fire-engines and the progress of the fire was stopped. But the whole of the Natural History Collection, the Assyrian, Byzantine and Alhambra Courts, the Queen's apartments, the library and printing offices, and a great deal of other valuable property, to the extent of between £200,000 and £300,000, was destroyed. Most of the unfortunate monkeys and live stock perished. One gentleman saved an eagle by carrying it away under his arm, and many other birds were set free. A day or two afterwards there was a snowstorm, and it is said that an extraordinary spectacle was presented by the remains of the

August Manns

huge models of Egyptian statues of Rameses the Great, 60 feet high, sitting charred and grim amid the desolation and ruin, their features and knees covered with snow.

Among the innumerable "interviews" granted by Manns there is one in which he relates that in the early days of the Palace he was commissioned by Ferguson, the manager, to engage Madame Rudersdorff for half a dozen concerts, and that the proposal met with a point-blank refusal by the artiste, on the ground that to sing at the Palace would injure her reputation. Her scruples must have been soon overcome, for her name frequently appears on the programmes in the years before the time we are now dealing with. It has recently been recalled to the memory of the public by the death of Mr. Richard Mansfield, the Anglo-American actor, who was her son.

At the Saturday Concert of March 17th, 1867, the overture to *Tannhaüser* was performed (it had been played there as early as April 1856), and provoked the critic of the *Sunday Times* to observe, "We cannot love the *Tannhaüser*, and shall be content with hearing it on occasions

Schubert's "Die Junge Nonne"

few and far between—just on those occasions
which the musical caterer, if he wish to promote
the progress of true music, will select for its
presentation. Even a nightmare may serve a
useful purpose if it tend to heighten our enjoy-
ment of waking fancies." At a succeeding
concert at which Clara Schumann and Edith
Wynne (1842-97) appeared, the latter sang
Schubert's "Die Junge Nonne," accompanied
by Arthur Sullivan, a selection from whose
Sapphire Necklace was first performed on the
same occasion.

At the end of the 1866-67 season the Directors,
as was frequently their custom, gave the audience
a review of the past season, specifying the works
and artistes which had been presented to the
public. It is far too lengthy to be given here,
but, as we have seen, it included a great deal of
the orchestral music of Schubert which had
never been heard in England. The "Unfinished
Symphony" was played for the first time on April
6th, and Mendelssohn's "Reformation Symphony"
later in the year, and a large quantity of music
by native composers made its first appearance,

August Manns

including works by Sterndale Bennett, Macfarren, and the fine "In Memoriam" overture by Sullivan.

The artistes, besides those already mentioned, who appeared during the season were Arabella Goddard, Joachim (1831-1907), Ludvig Strauss, Sainton, Piatti (1822-1901), Dannreuther (1844-1905), Hartvigson, and Franklin Taylor.

The judicious comment of the *Times* critic at the close of the season was that, while still "unable to sympathize with the enthusiasm of Herr Manns for the compositions of Robert Schumann, it is impossible not to respect his motives in bringing so many of them before the public." At the end of the season the same writer handsomely acknowledged that the 1866-67 season had been the most brilliant ever known at the Palace, having comprised "a succession of orchestral performances without parallel in this country and unsurpassed in any other. Never in England . . . have the symphonies of Beethoven been performed as under the direction of Herr Manns at the Crystal Palace."

The following list of the *personnel* of the band of players comprising the famous orchestra

Overture to " Semiramide "

about this time is compiled[1] by the aid of Mr. George Webb, the only surviving member of the orchestra with whom the writer has been able to get into touch :—

Van Heddeghem (leader), Vogel and T. Watson (first violins), Isaac Collins, father of Viotti Collins (second violin), Stehling and T. Reynolds (tenors), W. Reed ('cello), Biehl (double bass), Alfred Wells (flute), Crozier (oboe), Pape (clarinet), George Webb (second clarinet), Hutchins (bassoon), Levy and Duhem (cornets), Eckhoff (horn), and Thompson (timpani).

In the programme of 26th October 1867, there is a long preliminary note to Rossini's overture to *Semiramide*, signed " A. M.," in which the writer describes the plot of the opera in some detail and finishes his synopsis thus :—

" Does the overture lead any one to anticipate the presence of these events ? Does any one hear in its

[1] It is unfortunate that, as stated elsewhere in this work, no copy of the earliest programmes can now be found, and the pay-sheets have been destroyed, so that it is to be feared a complete list can hardly be reconstructed.

pretty and sparkling bravura melodies anything of
the hidden passions of a queen who has poisoned
her husband, is brought into contact with his ghost,
and finally killed by her own son within the very
tomb of her murdered spouse? To my feelings this
favourite prelude seems rather to have for its motto,
"Freut euch des Lebens" (Life let us cherish),
as, indeed, its principal subject is extremely like
that old German song, and it is not unlikely
that the thoroughly joyous character of the work
has largely ministered towards its great popularity."

On November 9th, 1867, Manns introduces an
overture (to *Prometheus*, op. 16) by Bargiel, a young
fellow-countryman of his, to the Palace audiences,
with many kindly words of commendation. He
prefaces his remarks by mentioning that "musical
Germany classes him amongst the most worthy
of its young composers," and concludes thus:
"A work which aims so high as this overture
must necessarily appear diffuse at a first hearing,
but I can bear witness that it becomes quite
clear and intelligible music of undeniable merit
when sufficiently known.—A. M."

In the programme for the following week, the

Schubert's "Rosamunde"

14th, the analytical remarks to Schubert's Symphony in C Major (No. 9) are for the first time signed by the famous [G], to whose eloquent word-painting and searching criticism the Palace audiences were and are so deeply indebted for the light they throw upon the great masterpieces of Beethoven, Mozart, Handel, Mendelssohn, Schumann, and Schubert.

An interesting reference to this season in Mr. Bennett's *Forty Years of Music* runs thus:—

"I have already recalled the vogue of Schubert in 1867-68, when work after work unheard of before in this country was produced at the Palace with loving care, and received with fervent admiration, . . . for it seemed to us that the shining glass-house at Sydenham had become the temple of a new and gracious gospel. . . . At this time, and for many years after, the Crystal Palace Concerts flourished as though nothing could extinguish, or even dim, the 'vital spark' which burned within them. They stood firm as the Pyramids, and we never dreamed for them an evil time."

On March 28th, 1868, four of the long-missing portions (*q.v.*) of Schubert's *Rosamunde* music

August Manns

were first performed before an English audience. On the 2nd April, Edward Lloyd made his first appearance at the Crystal Palace. On the 4th April, Mr. J. F. Barnett conducted the new cantata, *The Ancient Mariner*, which he had written for the Birmingham Festival of August 1867; and during the same months Manns continued his unwavering support of Sullivan by bringing forward his Symphony in E a second time, and by including in a concert his part-song, then newly-written but now almost a classic, " O hush thee, my Babie."

About midway through the following season, 1868-69, Manns rendered notable service to the Palace Company and Sir Michael Costa, although his hands were indeed more than sufficiently full of the work of an extremely onerous period, replete with new productions. A Rossini Festival had been announced for May 1869, under the auspices of the Sacred Harmonic Society, with Costa as conductor. At the last moment he fell ill, and was unable to take some, or, indeed, any of the most important rehearsals. The directors called upon their faithful music-director and with the

Benefit Concert

happiest results; he responded in his typical strenuous fashion, and the festival was a great success. Nor were the thanks of the directors limited to words. On the 7th May 1869 he received a characteristically genial and pleasant letter from his friend Grove, conveying "a cheque for £115, being half of the profit derived from the benefit concert on the 24th April, with the directors' compliments and best wishes." The letter finishes thus:—

I take this opportunity of conveying the thanks of the Board for your valuable services in conducting the rehearsals for the Rossini Festival during the absence of Sir Michael Costa, and for the manner in which you undertook the great extra labour consequent thereon.

I am, my dear Manns,

Yours ever sincerely,

G. GROVE,

August Manns, Esq.   *Secretary.*

During the year 1868 there was gathering to a head the long-fomenting discontent of those connected with orchestral performances with the

August Manns

high pitch that had been introduced into England by Sir M. Costa. Manns threw himself into the fray with his customary energy, and was one of the first to advocate the impossibility of retaining the high pitch. He published a leaflet advocating the reduction by a full half-tone, and suggesting a conference of band-conductors on this very important subject. It was not, however, until 1895, a period of twenty-six years later, that the leading orchestral society of the kingdom, the Philharmonic, officially set the example of lowering the pitch to the "normal diapason," which is now almost universally adopted in England by all bands.

Mr. Graves has an interesting note in his *Life of Grove*, relating that on August 12th, 1868, a choice little *partie carrée* dined together, consisting of Grove, Sullivan, Manns, and Ferdinand David (1810-73), the distinguished violinist, who illustrated the advance in technical accomplishment by the following remark: " When I began to play there were some pieces, such as Lipinski's 'Military Concerto' and Ernst's 'Hungarian Fantasia,' which only two or three men in

Bennett's G Minor Symphony

Europe could play. Now all my pupils play them."

A performance of Sterndale Bennett's G Minor Symphony (op. 43), on Saturday, 5th March 1870, brought the following letter from the composer:—

March 10th, 1870.

My dear Mr. Manns,

I hope you will not think me cold and indifferent as to the introduction of my Symphony in the Crystal Palace programme last Saturday. I could not be there because I was obliged to give a lecture at Cambridge, one of a series in the university programme. One of my sons was there and some other near relations, and they all told me how beautifully the work was played. *Many thanks to you.*

I shall do myself the pleasure of sending you a score of my Overture of *Paradise and the Peri*, which is just published at Leipzig, if you will accept it. Believe me,

Yours always faithfully,

WILLIAM STERNDALE BENNETT.

A. Manns, Esq.

95

August Manns

In 1870, Manns' powers were taxed to their utmost with the work entailed by the Beethoven Centenary Celebration. It is not possible to do more than glance at the tremendous programmes, the joint work of Grove and Manns, which were set before the audiences.

The whole of Beethoven's greatest works were performed at a series of twelve concerts, from October 1st to December 17th. The nine Symphonies, played in numerical order, the five Piano Concertos, the Violin Concerto, the Overtures to *Prometheus, Egmont, Coriolanus, Leonora* (Nos. 1, 2, and 3), *Fidelio,* and a mass of other great works was played, and the "Liederkreis" sung by Sims Reeves, with Arthur Sullivan playing the accompaniments.

Nor were other composers forgotten during these stupendous performances, for Sullivan's "Ouverture di Ballo" was heard for the first time (on 1st October), and Gounod and Ferdinand Hiller conducted symphonies.

CHAPTER IV.

A FURTHER increase in salary had marked the
directors' appreciation of Manns' services the year
before, when for the second time his friend Grove
had the gratifying task of writing officially to him
as follows:—

April 11th, 1871.

MY DEAR SIR,

I have the pleasure to inform you that at the
last board the question of your remuneration was
brought before the Directors, and that it was unanimously resolved to increase the same from £500 to
£600 a year, commencing from the 1st of September
last.

I am glad to inform you that the resolution was
accompanied by many expressions on the part

August Manns

of the Directors of confidence in you and satisfaction at the result of your labours.

Yours faithfully,

(Signed) G. GROVE,

Secretary.

During the next season (1871-72), similar
herculean labours were in store for Manns. The
Beethoven Festival had proved so great an
attraction that a Mendelssohn Commemoration
on similar lines was planned. Space fails to
allow a description, or even a complete list, of the
works performed, which were, as far as possible,
arranged in a chronological order.

At that time he lived with his family at
Balham, in a house adjoining St. Mary's Church
in the High Road. Not satisfied with the
volume of regular work that fell to his lot, he
undertook for a short time the training of the
boys of the choir at the church close by, his
devotion even extending to joining them in the
choir seats on Sundays. This, however, cannot
have continued long, for the inconvenient train
service caused him to give up his Balham
residence and to move nearer the Palace.

Brahms' D Minor Concerto

In December 1872, Miss Agnes Zimmerman played Beethoven's rearrangement of his own Violin Concerto for the piano, " which appears to be a unique performance of an achievement by a great composer which is also unique."

On October 19th, 1872, the production of Professor Prout's Organ Concerto in E minor, and a similar work by Mr. Henry Gadsby two years later, were both played by Dr. Stainer.

In March 1872, Brahms' Piano Concerto in D minor, op. 15, was heard for the first time in England at the Palace. Nine years before, but not since then, a work of the great Hungarian musician had been included in a Palace programme. In 1873 and 1874 several of his more important works were introduced to the English public, setting an example soon followed by the Philharmonic Society, and once again laying musical England under a heavy debt to August Manns.

The letter subjoined bears no date of year, but it serves to show how thoroughly Manns kept in touch with the great modern composers, whose works he was constantly producing:—

August Manns

DEAR SIR,

Herr Joachim has just forwarded your letter to me, which I hasten to answer. Unfortunately, it is impossible for me to comply with your wish, and I hope you will believe me when I tell you how particularly I regret my inability to do so towards yourself. My conductor's duties here last also from October 18th to the end of April, and I cannot well be absent for a fortnight on account of the Chorus rehearsals and preparations for the Concerts.

I should like to take this opportunity of telling you what great pleasure it gives me to know of the warm interest which you take in my music, and to hear through my friends of your excellent performances of the same. I therefore regret the more, as I said before, that my position here does not permit me to take this journey.

With the greatest esteem,

Your most humble servant,

J. BRAHMS.[2]

---

[1] This letter bears no date of year.
[2] Original German :—

September 7th.

GEEHRTESTER HERR,—Herr Joachim ubersandte mir soeben Ihren Brief u. ich eile darauf zu antworten. Leider

Andante to Mozart's "Parisian"

In March 1873, there was performed a new MS. Andante written by Mozart for his "Parisian" Symphony and intended to be an improvement on the original one. In November of the same year Hans von Bülow (1830-94) made his first appearance at Sydenham. During the season Frederick Cowen conducted a composition of his own at the Palace, and in February Joachim played Brahms' "Hungarian Dances," accompanied by Franklin Taylor, while the same composer's *Schicksalslied* was first produced in March and was immediately repeated by request.

At the end of the 1873-74 season there was, as

ist es mir versagt Ihrem freundlichen Wunsch nachkommen zu können u. ich bitte zu glauben dass ich dieses gerade Ihnen gegenüber ganz besonders bedauere. Auch *meine* Direktions Thätigkeit währt gerade vom 13 October bis letzten April und Kann ich in dieser Zeit doch nicht wohl 14 Tage verreisen der wöchentlichen [chorübungen] wegen.

Ich möchte doch bei dieser Gelegenheit Ihnen ausspre- chen wie grosse Freude es mir macht von Ihrem warmen Interesse für meine Musik zu wissen und von meinen Freunden über Ihre vortreffliche Aufführungen zu hören. Um so mehr bedauere ich wie gesagt, dass meine Stellung mir nicht erlaubt jene Reise zu machen.

In ausgezeichneter Hochachtung,

Ihr ergebener,

J. BRAHMS.

August Manns

usual, a benefit concert arranged for the conductor. In connection therewith he received the following letter, typical of the generous and true artistic spirit Sims Reeves always maintained towards August Manns and his other professional colleagues throughout a long and brilliant career:—

GRANGE MOUNT,

BEULAH SPA, NORWOOD,

April 14*th*, 1874.

MY DEAR MANNS,

I am so much better (in spite of the trying weather) that I feel justified in gratifying the wish I have so long indulged in to offer my services on the occasion of your benefit, as a mark of sympathy as regards our beloved art and personal regard for one who has done his work so bravely and conscientiously. It is not much I offer, but the offer is freely made.

With much hope for a glorious success,

Yours sincerely,

J. SIMS REEVES.

August Manns always set his face sternly

"Tinkering with the Classics"

against any "tinkering with the classics," and the programme of this benefit concert (on 25th April 1874) contains a characteristic contribution from the conductor's pen on a kindred subject which then engaged some attention in the musical papers. The controversy was started in the *Monthly Musical Record* of the 1st April, in which an article, signed "C. A. B.," criticized Manns adversely for a performance of Beethoven's Choral Symphony without the adoption of Wagner's suggestions for a modification of the instrumentation of certain passages. Manns enumerates briefly the suggestions as follows:—

1. Modifications of nuances in order to secure a distinct production of the melodic element.

2. Recommendations for adding horns and chromatic trumpets to the well-known melody in the Scherzo for which Beethoven has employed wood instruments only (Breitkopf's full Score, page 77).

3. Recommendations for letting the violins and flute play in several bars an octave higher than written in the grand part of the Scherzo (Breitkopf's full Score, page 91).

August Manns

4. Suggestions for altering the melodic phrases in the wood instruments in those well-known eight bars of the first movement at pp. 19 and 53 of Breitkopf's full Score.

5. Recommendations for altering the tenor part in the Vocal Quartett in B natural, page 265 full Score.

" C. A. B.'s" article concludes thus :—

" It remains, therefore, for conductors to decide whether it is better to continue the practice of presenting Beethoven's works as they stand or to adopt such emendations as Wagner has proposed, the writer being fully convinced that the time was not far distant when they will be regarded as much a *sine quâ non* as Mozart's additional accompaniments to the *Messiah.*"

Manns' answer was characteristically vigorous, and is here fully reproduced :—

" In replying on the present occasion to 'C. A. B.' I would first call his attention to the absence of all parallel between the case of Mozart's additions to Handel and Wagner's emendations of Beethoven, inasmuch as the scores of Handel were left in a

Answer to "C. A. B."

deplorably incomplete state as regards the modern orchestra, whereas those of Beethoven are in every way complete productions. In the second place, I beg to assure him that I belong to those who are always willing to learn, and that I therefore procured a copy of Wagner's pamphlet as soon as I knew of its existence; and next, I will state why I have not followed the suggestions it contains :—

1. The modifications of nuances needed no special pointing out, for every conductor who possesses the necessary talent and culture for his post knows but too well that a goodly number of scores by the older masters require these modifications, in consequence of the larger number of strings we are compelled to employ in our larger concert-rooms.

2. The suggestion for reinforcing Beethoven's melodies for wood instruments by horns and piston-trumpets I repudiate *in toto*, because the classic colouring of the author's original would be vulgarized, if not wholly destroyed.

3. The suggestion for letting the first violins and flute play portions of their parts an octave

August Manns

higher I hesitate to adopt, because I do not wish to bring that impure intonation into Beethoven's Symphony which, in consequence of an undue demand on the capabilities of the executants made by many composers of our day, is such an unpleasant feature whenever their works are produced.

4. The suggested alterations of the eight bars for wind-instruments in the first movement are quite unwarrantable, and Wagner's analysis is here entirely wrong. The principal characteristic of this agitated tone group of eight bars is close imitation, both tonically and metrically, of the first four notes of the subject. Wagner's extraordinary alterations, which require actually omissions of parts in order to fit his views, destroy that characteristic tonically almost entirely.

5. The recommendation to allow the solo tenor part in the Quartett in B major must have sprung from Wagner's presence at some German festival long ago, at which the solos were sung by amateurs. The part in question is, no doubt, troublesome, but has

Gounod

been sung in England over and over again most satisfactorily.

" ' C. A. B.' must therefore, I fear, continue to express his surprise. At any rate, he must forego the pleasure of hearing Wagner's Beethoven at the Crystal Palace as long as the direction of the musical department is confided to myself, and I trust that all who may follow me may at least agree with me in this, that Beethoven's works require no such alterations as are suggested by Herr Wagner, considered as they are by all, except a small minority, as the most perfect monuments of musical art in existence.

A. MANNS."

Among the few existing letters from the many great composers with whom Manns must have corresponded there is the following from Gounod (1818-93), which is at least interesting in its revelation of the composer's perfect mastery of English. It is dated from the house wherein the illustrious Frenchman was then staying in London, and in which Charles Dickens resided from 1851-60:—

August Manns

MY DEAR MR. MANNS,

If you can manage to insert my new song in one of the two programmes of June it would greatly oblige me, as we shall most certainly leave London for July and August. Now, as regards the French sacred music (new music) I could not tell you anything, as I did not witness the musical movement in France in this way for a few years.

You'll perhaps tell me that I am *orfèvre*,[1] if I mention my own latest sacred work, the Mass *SS. Angeli and Eustache* (*sic*), which includes an Orchestral Communion March, and also the new Orchestral Offertory added to the new edition of my *Messe Solennelle;* both of which (Offertory and Communion March) have been *encored* at my orchestral concerts, and would be lent to you, if wanted, of course gratuitously. I suppose you know Ad. Adam's very well-known *Marche réligieuse*. As regards dramatic music, I keep at your disposal the short but always effective introduction

---

[1] Literally, "a usurer."

Ouseley's "Hagar"

of my *Jeanne d'Arc*. I am quite strange to ball-room music, and couldn't give you any hint about it.

Believe me, dear Mr. Manns,

Yours most sincerely,

CH. GOUNOD.

In November 1874, Raff's "Lenore" Symphony, since become one of the most popular at the Palace, was first performed.

In December 1874, a performance of Ouseley's (1825-89) *Hagar* elicited the following letter from the composer:—

TENBURY,

December 22nd, 1874.

MY DEAR SIR,

I could not find time till to-day to write and thank you, as I now do most heartily, for the evident pains and care you took in getting up the performance of *Hagar* last Saturday. It is the fourth time it has been done, and it never was so thoroughly well done before. I can truly say that on the whole I was delighted and that I feel much gratified.

Believe me,

Yours very truly and obliged,

FREDK. A. GORE-OUSELEY.

August Manns

Among the pleasantest experiences of Manns' career were the frequent and substantial tokens he received of the affection he inspired among all those brought into contact with him. The year 1875 brought one of those charming occasions with it in the presentation of a silver tea and coffee service from the members of the Crystal Palace Choir.

The two years following may be briefly referred to. The early months of 1875 were saddened for all English musicians by the death of Sterndale Bennett, to whose consummate art Manns and his orchestra ever rendered the homage of perfect interpretation. Edward Dannreuther and Oscar Beringer introduced some new piano concertos, including an early work of Hubert Parry. More than once the names of other English composers appear, notably that of John Francis Barnett, who had played there as a boy nearly twenty years before, and who now conducted, not, however, for the first time, a Concerto of his own composition.

In 1877 Rubinstein, perhaps the greatest of modern pianists, appeared at the Palace twice, the second time coming to Manns' benefit concert at the end of the season to conduct his humoresque, "Don Quixote."

On December 12th, 1877, Cimarosa's cele-brated comic opera, *The Secret Marriage*, was performed at the Palace in English, by per-mission of Mr. D'Oyly Carte and under the superintendence of Mr. Richard Temple, who himself had made his début at the Palace in an opera performance in 1869. The cast included Miss Florence St. John, who had then only two years before made her début on the London music-hall stage at a *matinée*, where she sang Sullivan's "Meet me Once Again." The orchestra was directed by Manns.

During the early 'seventies the Crystal Palace Theatre became famous for the brilliant revivals of many old comedies under the direction of Charles Wyndham, with whom Manns formed a friendship which lasted throughout his life.

Later in the year two other world-famed musicians, Sarasate and Max Bruch, were invited by Manns to the Palace, the one to play and

August Manns

the other to conduct the celebrated Violin Concerto (op. 26).

In 1877, Manns had the, for him, unusual and unpleasant experience of an unprovoked attack from the eccentric genius, von Bülow, who in the columns of a paper now extinct, the *London Figaro*, made some unaccountable statements about his conducting powers and general behaviour. Manns requested an explanation, and as none was forthcoming, took the somewhat ill-advised course of issuing a pamphlet entitled "Dr. Hans von Bülow's Prescriptions for the Cure of Anti-Bülowism." His antagonist, however, still refused to be drawn, and this state of things continued for three or four years, until one evening at the opera Manns received a note on a card which ran thus:—"Hans von Bülow begs, though somewhat late, to thank Herr Musik-director Manns for the honour which he has so generously conferred upon the 16th sin of his youth." The reference was to a performance a short time previously of his opus 16, a clever orchestral ballad, "The Curse of the Minstrel." This communica-

Walter Bache

tion caused Manns to regard the quarrel as terminated.

Nothing is more pleasantly certain than that the reproach of ingratitude so often levelled against mankind was not exemplified in the relationship between Manns and those English composers he befriended. The letter from Walter Bache (1842-88) subjoined is a typical instance:—

42 UPPER GLOUCESTER PLACE,

DORSET SQUARE, N.W.,

February 20*th*, 1878.

DEAR MR. MANNS,

I will not attempt to write you a letter of thanks, but I am none the less conscious of what I owe you for your kindness last night. I shall write to Liszt next Sunday, send him a programme, and tell him I think the *Orpheus* performance was a *most admirable* one—it was in every way first-rate, and that the whole performance was one with which he would have been pleased.

Yours ever sincerely,

WALTER BACHE.

August Manns

According to Constance Bache's *Brother Musicians*, in which she gives the memoirs of her brother Walter, the concert mentioned in this letter was on February 19th, 1878, and was given by Walter Bache at St. James's Hall, with August Manns conducting. The concert contained chiefly works of Liszt, amongst others his *Orpheus*.

Later in the season Max Bruch sent the following letter appreciative of a performance of one of his works at the Palace:—

11 Ryder Street,

St. James',

Whit-Monday, '78.

Dear Mr. Manns,

All my time to-day and to-morrow being filled up, and as I unfortunately must leave for the Continent on Wednesday, I fear that I will be unable to shake hands with you again before I start on my journey. In any case, I send these lines to bid you farewell and to express to you the pleasure it has afforded me to have been once more enabled to work together with you musically.

Massenet

And I must tell you that I greatly appreciate the fact that you, besides your *well*-known and *well*-recognized merits as orchestral conductor, have added those of *choir*-leader and choir-*singer*, and I therefore must dedicate a special word of praise to the *Choir-master* A. Manns! You remind me of F. Weber in Cologne; he could also sing alto, tenor or bass, just as it was required.

Everything went *splendidly*. Even the difficult passage "Ashes," to which I, unfortunately, could not devote sufficient time at the rehearsal in the morning, went much better than I ever expected it would go—probably due to your assistance.

Yours faithfully,

MAX BRUCH.

In March 1878, Sullivan's song, "The Lost Chord," was sung by Signor Foli with immense effect. In May of this year the French composer, Massenet, visited the Palace and conducted selections from his *Le Roi de Lahore*. During this season, also, the names of Villiers Stanford and Parry are again brought into prominence, the former by a MS. Symphony in B flat, and the latter by an Overture. Scharwenka also added

August Manns

to the extraordinary brilliance of the season by playing a composition of his own and Weber's Concertstück.

In February 1879, another illustrious musician's name was first brought before the audiences at the Crystal Palace by August Manns. Dr. Shinn remarks on the difficulty of realizing that so lately as this the name of Anton Dvörák (1841-1904) was unknown in England, or, indeed, anywhere but in his native country. The note appended in the programme to his famous "Sclavonic Dances" (op. 46), which first introduced him here, states that "so little is it [his name] known, even in Germany, that it has been found impossible to obtain any information as to his position and antecedents, or the nature of his works, which, it will be observed, have reached their 46th opus." He did not appear before the public of his own country till 1873, nor was it till four years later that, by the friendly offices of Brahms, he was commissioned to write a series of Sclavonic Dances as pianoforte duets, by Simrock, the Berlin publisher. These were the compositions performed at the

Dvŏrák

Palace in 1879; but not until five years later, when his name was becoming increasingly well known, did the great Bohemian musician come in person to the Palace. That he was not insensible of the valuable services Manns rendered him is shown by the following letter, written before his first visit to this country:—

PRAG,

10/9/83.

DEAR MR. MANNS,

Although I returned from my summer holiday in Vysoka some three weeks ago, I have been unable to answer your kind letter until now. Before all I feel I must tender you the thanks which I owe to you since a long time, for your very kind efforts and the trouble you have taken in bringing my music before the English public, especially in London.[1] I therefore now venture to draw your attention to the very newest of my works, consisting of a Violin Concerto, op. 53, published this

---

[1] Many of the foreign artists think that the Crystal Palace is *in* London if they have not been here. At the time when Dvorák wrote this I think he had not yet been to London.

August Manns

year by Simrock in Berlin, and the following, which
are in preparation at the publishers, Bote & Bock:—
Nocturne for strings, op. 40, a short piece playing
6-7 minutes; also a large orchestral work, Scherzo
Capriccioso, op. 66. If you care to include one or
other of these pieces in your programmes, I should
be delighted.

Thanking you in anticipation,

I remain,

Yours very sincerely,

A. DVŎRÁK.[1]

---

[1] Original German:—

PRAG, 10/9/83.

SEHR GEEHRTER HERR MANNS, — Schon seit drei
Wochen von meinem Sommeraufenthalte Vysoka verreist
bin ich erst jetzt in der angenehmen Lage Ihnen zu antworten *
Vor Allem muss ich Ihnen den längst schüldigen Dank
sagen für Ihre liebevolle Mühe und Bestrebung meine
Werke in England namentlich in London bekannt gemacht
zu rathen, und ich es jetzt nicht unterlassen neue Sachen
von mir zu bringen. Ich erlaube mir also die neuesten
Erscheinungen in Kurze zu melden. Es sind ein violin
Konzert, op. 53, dieses Yahr bei Simrock in Berlin verlegt
dann im Drucke sind:—Nocturno für Streichorchester op.
40, ein kürzes Stück von 6-7 minuten dann ein grosses

Liszt's "The Battle of Huns"

In May 1879, there was a performance of Liszt's (1811-86) symphonic poem, "The Battle of the Huns," at the Palace, in connection with which the following letter was written. It is of interest as giving an authoritative statement of the origin of the work:—

WEIMAR,

May 25th, 1879.

DEAR SIR,

I must again beg you to excuse my delay in answering your letter. Fortunately, you yourself have come to the rescue with your commentary on my work, "The Battle of the Huns."

Kaulbach's world-famed picture represents two battles—the one on earth, the other in the air (or sky), according to the legend that the warriors

---

Orchesterstück Scherzo Capriccioso, op. 66, bei Bote und Bock in Berlin. Wenn sie vielleicht eins oder das andere in Ihr Programm aufnehmen wollen so würde mich dieses sehr freuen und sage ich Ihnen schon jetzt meinen verbin- lichsten Dank.

Hochachtungsvoll,

Ihr,

ANTONIN DVŎRÁK.

August Manns

continue to fight after their death, as spirits. In the centre of the picture the Cross is seen with its mysterious illumination, and upon this my Symphonic Poem is based. The chorale, "Crux fidelis," with its gradual development, expresses the idea of the final victory of Christianity in Love to God and man.

Thanking you for your kindly interest,

I remain,

Yours very sincerely,

F. LISZT.[1]

---

[1] Original German:—

WEIMAR,

25 *Mai* 1879.

SEHR GEEHRTER HERR,—Abermals muss ich sie bitten meine Schreibsäumnisse zu entschuldigen. Glücklicherweise haben sie selbst gut abgeholfen durch Ihren Kommentar der " Hunnenschlacht."

Kaulbach's weltberühmtes Bild führt zwei Schlachten vor; die eine auf Erdenboden, die andere in der Luft, gemäss der Legende dass die Krieger noch nach ihrem Tode als Gespenster unaufhaltsam fort kämpften. Inmitten des Bildes erscheint das Kreuz und sein geheimnissvolles Licht; daran haftet meine Symphonische Dichtung. Der sich allmählich entwickelnde Choral, " Crux fidelis," ver-

120

Glasgow Choral Union

In December of the same year the famous French musician, Camille Saint-Saëns, appeared both as a solo-pianist and as a conductor under Manns' friendly auspices.

In 1879 there came an invitation from the Glasgow Choral Union to become their conductor, and the best *resumé* of the yeoman service Manns rendered to music in Scotland is to be found in a speech addressed by Sir Donald Matheson to the guests at a complimentary banquet to the conductor on 21st January, 1895. He said :—

" It is fifteen years since Mr. Manns first came to Glasgow to succeed Sir Arthur Sullivan, Dr. von Bülow, and Herr Tausch as conductor of the orchestral concerts. . . . Mr. Manns but rarely takes engagements outside the Crystal Palace.

---

deutlicht die Idee des endlich siegenden Christenthums in wirksamer Liebe zu Gott und den Menschen.

Aufrichtig dankend für Ihre wohlwollende Gesinnung,

Verbleibt Ihnen,

Ergebenst,

F. LISZT.

August Manns

We were, therefore, fortunate in 1879 in securing his services. . . . These concerts, which grew out of the Musical Festival held in 1873, . . . had been in operation five years before the advent of Mr. Manns. Music-loving citizens of Glasgow had paid out through their guarantee funds a sum of over £4000, in order to keep the scheme going during these militant years. The Committee started with a series of sixteen concerts, which resulted in a loss of £2,300 the first year. When Mr. Manns came the season was reduced to ten concerts, and immediately a surplus appeared. During the whole time Mr. Manns has conducted these concerts surplus after surplus has accrued, until every penny of the old guarantee was refunded, and it was not until the last two or three seasons of Mr. Manns' conducting that we got into debt again. This arose, however, from circumstances over which our friend . . . had absolutely no control."

In March 1881, the second of those spontaneous expressions of popular esteem and the affection of his brother-musicians was offered to Manns. Under the presidency of Mr. Henry Leslie, a committee was formed and a sub-

Second Public Testimonial

scription list opened which speedily included the names of every musician of the day, whether amateur or professional. It is doubtful if any such completely universal testimonial of love and respect has been offered to any living man by his brethren in the craft as this and the other even greater demonstration in 1895.

On the present occasion we find the following among the first list of subscribers :—

Henry Leslie	F. H. Cowen
Henry Gadsby	A. H. D. Prendergast
C. E. Stephens	W. H. Cummings
W. Shakespeare	O. Beringer
Thos. Wingham	A. Randegger
Sims Reeves	F. Corder
Sir J. Benedict	E. J. Hopkins
C. Santley	J. Barnby
E. Silas	J. F. Bridge
G. Grove	A. Chappell
Walter Bache	G. A. Macfarren
Walter Macfarren	John Hullah
J. W. Davison	W. Kuhe
Franklin Taylor	Hubert Parry
E. Dannreuther	Villiers Stanford
J. F. Barnett	Arthur Sullivan
E. Prout	C. A. Barry

August Manns

and a host of others too numerous to mention. In all, a sum of about £800 was collected, and the presentation was made by the late Sir George Macfarren, on June 17th, 1882. The names of the subscribers (581 in all) were inscribed in an album with the following inscription :—

" Presented to AUGUST MANNS,

By Professor G. A. Macfarren, on behalf of the herein-mentioned subscribers, in recognition of his distinguished services to musical art, as specially instanced by his direction for upwards of a quarter of a century of the Saturday Concerts at the Crystal Palace, where the works of the great masters, as well as composers, both English and foreign, less known to fame, have been rendered in a manner which has redounded to his honour throughout the civilized world."

During the spring of 1881 Manns again met Rubinstein (1829-94), this time at St. James' Hall, when he was listening to a rehearsal of his " Dramatic Symphony." When the Scherzo was reached, in which the drum has a prominent part, he suddenly jumped up and said, " That

Sauret and Eugen d'Albert

drummer has no soul! Come and have some lunch." And walking up to the conductor, the late Sir William Cusins, he slapped him on the leg and said, " Cusins, I'm hungry—good-bye. Go on!" When after lunch, at which Carl Rosa was the third party, the waiter told him smoking was not allowed, he launched unexpectedly into a diatribe against English ladies. He was so bitter that Rosa asked him what he would do without them, and he replied, " Ah! dat is anoder matter. I would not care to live five minutes longer."

During the seasons of 1881-82 many distinguished musicians visited and played at the Palace. Sullivan conducted his *Martyr of Antioch*. Sauret, the violinist, and Eugen d'Albert both appeared, the latter being still a very young man. Tivadar de Nachez and Sophie Menter also made their Palace *débuts*. Among the remarkable works performed were Berlioz's (1803-69) *Symphonie Phantastique; or, Episode in the Life of an Artist*, and its sequel, *Lelio; or, the Return to Life*, both quite unknown in England.

August Manns

In May 1883, a yet more extraordinary performance took place of the same composer's *Grande Messe des Morts*, scored for an orchestra of 140—four small brass bands, eight pairs of kettle-drums, with ten drummers, two double drums, four "tamtams," ten pairs of cymbals, and requiring for its adequate performance of the six-part chorus a choir of 210 voices. The Crystal Palace Concert-room's accommodation would not quite permit of the full forces indicated by the composer being used, but the reduction in them was only slight. It is not surprising that this performance aroused such interest that a repetition of it was speedily announced.

During the previous season—to be precise, on the 28th October 1882—the prelude to Wagner's *Parsifal*—itself only then, as recently as July 26th, first brought into the world of music—was heard at the Palace. On the 13th February 1883, the great poet-musician himself died, and his memory was duly honoured at the Saturday Concerts by a complete "Wagner Concert." English music was not forgotten amidst the

Schubert's "No. 7" in E

prodigious performances of Berlioz and Wagner, Mackenzie, Parry, Wingham, and Cowen all contributing to its success. Mr. J. F. Barnett, greatly daring, conducted his version of the completed form of Schubert's Symphony No. 7 in E., from the MS. outline at that time in the possession of Sir George Grove.

The following letter from the then Principal of the Royal Academy of Music is not fully dated, but from the reference in the first paragraph to the presentation of a testimonial to Manns there can be little doubt of the year in which it was written:—

7 HAMILTON TERRACE, N.W.,

May 9th [1883].

MY DEAR MR. MANNS,

I am almost as pleased to receive your friendly greeting as I was last year to offer you my own, even though this included the good wishes of the multitude. Your name is recorded in a highly-prized list in relation to my birthday, and your autograph adds to the testimony of your

August Manns

friendship. The very much I owe you for often placing my music before the people, so as to make them believe that I merit my public compliment, is felt, although it cannot be said.

Yours faithfully,

G. MACFARREN.

CHAPTER V.

The illness of Sir M. Costa—Manns succeeds to the conductorship of the Handel Festival in 1883—Liszt in England—Joseph Bennett on Manns and his work—Grove at the Saturday Concerts—Handel Festivals 1885 and 1888—Letter of Thomas Wingham—Manns and Grove's tour to Bayreuth—Manns and Bernard Shaw—List of the orchestra 1888-89—The Handel Festival 1891—Manns receives a German decoration—Death of Mrs. Manns—Letter from Sir A. C. Mackenzie—The Handel Festival 1894—Manns becomes naturalized—Recollections of Manns by Mr. R. H. Walthew.

IF August Manns' life had been a busy one before 1883, after that year it was tenfold more so. Fortunately, his increased labours found him still a hale and hearty man, who, despite his grey hair and his fifty-eight years, was probably as fit to assume the herculean tasks yet in store as ever he had been in his life. For in that year Sir Michael Costa, the remarkable Italian musician who had raised himself from the position of an obscure tenor singer to the autocracy of the greatest opera-house in Europe, had a paralytic seizure. For very many years he had ruled the musical roost in England to an

August Manns

extraordinary extent. For twenty-six years he had dominated the Handel Festivals at the Crystal Palace. Under his rule they had, there is no doubt, attained a wonderful perfection. He had to a large extent sown the seed (and borne the heat and burden of doing so) of which Manns reaped the harvest. It is one thing to conceive and initiate the organization of a great under-taking, and another to step into the "driver's" place, pick up the reins, and guide the forces that have been collected.

It is no disparagement of the powers of August Manns to call attention to the fact that he took command of an extremely well-disciplined body when Costa became too ill to conduct the Festival of 1883;[1] and in saying this we have not overlooked the fact that as each triennium comes round some hundreds of new singers had to be heard, old ones weeded out, and the ever-increasing difficulty faced of finding a suitable

---

[1] Grove said of Costa:—"He was a splendid drill-sergeant; he brought the London orchestras into an order unknown before. He acted up to his lights, was thoroughly efficient as far as he went, and was eminently safe."

Handel Festival Conductor

programme upon Selection day, when Handelian novelties and rarities were looked for by the critics. But there was never the slightest doubt in the world as to his fitness for the post; it was his by every possible right.* He had attended every Festival since 1857, in itself no light achievement; and, as he told an interviewer many years later, "had fully studied the acoustic properties of the building, and could have given Sir Michael many hints." Manns never concealed his disagreement with many of his predecessor's methods. He is quoted as saying:—"His parts were full of cues, and it was more upon these than upon rehearsal that he relied for a successful performance." Manns' own method was to go through every note with the band first, and he was never satisfied with mere mechanical accuracy, but always aimed at and invariably succeeded in getting the effects he desired through strenuous practice. So it was no light task that he had assumed. The qualities demanded of a Handel Festival conductor are multifarious. His gifts must be many,

* See Appendix (2).

August Manns

his tact great, his physical and mental energy enormous. It has been said of Manns that to speak of him as the equal of Richter as a Wagner conductor, or of Barnby as a choir-trainer, would be the merest flattery; but he was indisputably the best all-round conductor of his day, and that was precisely the kind of man needed for the chief command of the Handel Festival.

Costa's personality had so impressed itself upon the Festivals that it had been freely prophesied that with his death they must die also. But the world knows better than this. We are none of us indispensable, and Sir Michael Costa was no exception. Almost at a few hours' notice—for Costa hoped up to the last to be well enough—Manns stepped into the vacant place. Some of the old chorus "hands," if we may be forgiven the expression, showed "mutinous inclinations" at the first choral rehearsal at Exeter Hall.

"But the new conductor restored good humour amongst his singers by practically demonstrating the pedestrian capabilities of Polyphemus by taking 'monstrous strides' across the platform, and singing

Congratulatory Epistles

the notes with Polyphemic gusto. He concluded
the final choral rehearsal with the following tactful
speech:—'Ladies and gentlemen, if you have as
much confidence in *me* as I have in *you*, we shall
have a great success.'"—*Musical Times*, March 1st,
1898.

It is now a matter of history that the 1883
Festival verified its conductor's prediction and
justified his methods. The curiosity and criticism
were, not unnaturally, keener than ever. The
financial receipts were the largest on record.
But it was unanimously agreed that the performances surpassed all previous efforts, and
were characterized by artistic finish never before
approached. It was incontestably a glorious
triumph for the conductor and all concerned,
and for days afterwards shoals of congratulatory
epistles were poured upon the modest but com-
fortable house at Dulwich Wood Park, where
the popular conductor lived.

Among the few of these which have been
carefully preserved is the following, in which it
is evident that Manns took peculiar pleasure:—

August Manns

CRYSTAL PALACE, SYDENHAM,

June 1883.

To A. MANNS, Esq.

DEAR SIR,

We, the undersigned members of the Royal Italian Opera, Covent Garden, and extras of the orchestra of the Crystal Palace Saturday Concerts, desire to send you a few lines of sympathy in connection with your arduous duties of last week, and our honest admiration of the manner in which the conducting of the orchestra of the Handel Festival was begun, continued, and finished by you. And we desire you to accept these few words in the spirit that prompted them, and also to add our hearty wishes and hopes that we may see you in the same position on the recurrence of the Handel Festival. With our united kind regards and best wishes for your continued success.

We beg to remain,

Yours faithfully,

S. VON PRAAG.	EDWIN OULD.
A. G. STREATHER.	W. W. WAUD.
SAMUEL R. WEBB.	THOMAS LAWRENCE.
JOHN BOATWRIGHT.	H. T. TRUST.
VIOTTI COLLINS.	ELLIS ROBERTS.
J. EARNSHAW.	J. J. JAKEWAY.

Press Notices

If it were possible to quote even a tithe of the glowing press notices that followed this great achievement, some idea might be gained of the success Manns had attained. The bare figures, stupendous though they are, convey so little to a reader. The 4000 picked performers drawn from all parts of the country, the 440 instrumentalists, formed, as one famous critic put it, "the greatest musical machine of all time. . . . The vast mass moved with well-nigh perfect precision, took up every point with accuracy . . . and made Englishmen proud of the musical resources of their country." But it is impossible to linger any more upon this part of Manns' career, important though it be. We shall find him, as each triennial festival comes round, renewing the laurels he had so worthily won.

The welcome routine of the Saturday Concerts had to be pursued. March 22nd, 1884, was a notable date, for Dvořák visited the Palace and conducted some of his works in person.

On October 25th, the annual performance of Schubert's C major Symphony brought the

August Manns

following notice from Grove, contributed to the
Pall Mall Gazette :—

" Mr. Manns took the Finale a shade slower
than usual, and it was possibly due to this fact
that its impetuosity and enormous force were
shaded with an awful supernatural cast, never
before apparent. It was as if the tremendous
conflict or drama depicted by the music were
taking place somewhere outside the world, and as
if the inhabitants of the earth were regarding it
awestruck, longing, but powerless to help."

On 8th November of the same year, being
the beginning of the following season, Madame
Antoinette Trebelli made her first appearance at
the Palace. Later in the month Sir Alexander
Mackenzie's *Rose of Sharon* was performed,
under the bâton of the composer. In February
and March 1885, two Historical Concerts were
arranged, to illustrate the progress of instrumental music. The first was entirely devoted
to the German composers—Bach, Mendelssohn,
and Brahms. The second extended from an
Italian composer who flourished in 1557 to

Liszt in England

The Valkyrie's Ride of Wagner, comprehending between these two, excerpts from Purcell, Handel, Bach, Haydn, Mozart, and Beethoven.

In October 1885, Frederick Corder's Concert Overture, *Prospero*, was produced.

In 1886 the famous visit of the Abbé Liszt to England took place. He stayed, it will be remembered, with the late Mr. Henry Littleton, of Westwood House, Sydenham, and was therefore in close proximity to the Palace, where so much of his greatest work had been first brought before the public. He naturally saw a good deal of Manns, who arranged that the two concerts which occurred during his visit should be devoted entirely to his works. Liszt was himself present at them, and at the rehearsal for them.

" In the interpretation of the several works Mr. Manns' splendid orchestra surpassed itself. The players to a man were thoroughly on their mettle, determined to let the Abbé know what an English orchestra could do, and the result was a magnificent performance. Even Liszt himself could not but

137

August Manns

acknowledge this,[1] and from his place in the front row of seats immediately beneath the conductor's desk he more than once rose to shake Mr. Manns cordially by the hand and to bow to the audience, whose cheers and applause reverberated throughout the enclosed area."—*Musical Times*, 1886.

In the evening Manns again met his great fellow-countryman at the German Athenæum, and later in the same day and for the next two or three weeks the famous musician was the lion of London, until his departure on Thursday, April 22nd.

On the Saturday previous to his departure he again honoured the concert-room by his presence to hear his *St. Elizabeth* produced under the bâton of Dr. Mackenzie, and it is said that on this occasion the venerable composer yielded to the soporific influence of the concert-room and fell asleep while listening to his own music!

---

[1] In speaking of the performance afterwards, Liszt said to Manns: "Ich wusste doch nicht bis heute dasz ich so schön componirt hätte." ("I did not know till to-day that I had written such beautiful music.")

English Music

During May 1886, Manns aroused great interest by his masterly handling of orchestra and chorus in a performance of Gounod's *Redemption*, for the first time at the Crystal Palace.

In October 1886, Ella Russell made her first appearance at the Palace, and there was a memorial concert to the illustrious composer whose presence but six short months before the Palace audience had acclaimed. Dr. Shinn does well to emphasize in his pamphlet the remarkable consistency of Manns' efforts to encourage English music. To a man of his kindness of heart no part of his duty can have been more irksome or uncongenial than the sifting and rejection of the piles of music submitted for his inspection week in and week out throughout the year. But his reward was certain if the process of search was laborious.

In an appreciative article by Joseph Bennett, on January 30th, 1895, adverting to this part of Manns' work, the writer remarks:—

" Throughout his career he has never examined works aspiring to his favour with anything but an eye to excellence. In all schools of music good is

August Manns

to be found. Mr. Manns has looked for, discovered, and helped the good without reference to
the school. . . . The Englishman stands as fair a
chance as the foreigner, and the half-forgotten
worthies of the eighteenth century are as likely to
have their value admitted as the more generally
recognized composers of our own time. This is
much to say at a period when musical likes and
dislikes are strong, and it is this which has made
the Crystal Palace Concerts a great educational
force in the broadest sense."

Many of the English names that have occurred
in our abstract and brief chronicle had won
recognition in other directions partly from the
" hall-mark " conferred upon them by a Crystal
Palace performance.

In 1885 another and a younger school of
composers began to arise, among them Hamish
McCunn, whose cantata, *Lord Ullin's Daughter*,
was performed in 1887, and for whose " Land of
the mountain and the flood " Manns had an
extraordinary admiration.

When Grove left the Crystal Palace in
September 1873 much of his intimate associa-

tion with August Manns was of necessity discontinued, but he remained, of course, as writer of the famous notes in the programmes, and seldom failed to attend the concerts, with a band of chosen friends, in some seats in the gallery. Upon his appointment in 1882 as Director of the newly-formed Royal College of Music, he had, naturally, wished to retain the services of his old friend and colleague in his new sphere, and a way was found by appointing him an examiner to the College, in which capacity he continued to act for many years.* It is perhaps worthy of note that the letters received by the examiners annually informing them of the probable date their services would be required were signed by the royal President himself. No light proof this of the keenness of his present Majesty in the furtherance of any project in which he takes an interest.

To revert for a moment to Grove's connection with the concerts, a charming reminiscence is related on page 292 of his *Life* by Mr. Graves:—

---

* See Appendix (3).

August Manns

" Grove very soon started the practice, which
he maintained throughout his Directorship, of
organizing parties of pupils for the Crystal Palace
Concerts, where he might be seen, Saturday after
Saturday throughout the season, in his seat at the
back of the gallery, the centre of a group of his
' children,' with a full score in his lap, pointing out
his favourite passages and leading the applause.
When the concert was over there was generally a
tea-party at a special table, where ' G ' was at his
best, discussing the concert, telling anecdotes, and
generally radiating sunshine."

A Handel Festival had been held in June 1885,
(in order to coincide with the bi-centenary of
Handel's birth), which was twelve months in
advance of the ordinary course of the Festivals.
On this occasion nearly 1000 new voices were
engaged, and the number and scope of the
rehearsals increased.   Sir Michael Costa was
not accustomed to rehearse the *Messiah*, which
Manns did as thoroughly as everything else.
The chorus was slightly smaller and the band
larger than usual.   The public attendance showed
no sign of falling off, and the severest critics could

find but few faults with the brilliant success of Manns, now firmly fixed in his new position. The next Festival was that of 1888, which showed the same tendency to improvement, both artistically and financially, that had marked its predecessors. There were still—and Manns was proud of the fact—many of the singers in the chorus who had sung in the Festivals of 1857 and 1859. Several highly interesting novelties were performed on Selection Day, including choruses from *Belshazzar*, *Alexander Balus*, and the Ninety-fifth Psalm. The labour of preparing the programmes occupied the conductor for many weeks before the Festival, not to mention the journeys into the country to rehearse the contingents from provincial towns. In one of the interviews which Manns granted to Press representatives he remarks on the immense progress he had noticed in English choral singing generally during the previous ten years. The Bradford and Leeds contingent, for example, sang their parts at rehearsals so admirably that no criticism was needed.

The 1888 Festival was the occasion of an ill-

August Manns

timed political demonstration directed against Mr. Gladstone, who was present.

During the season 1887-88 new works by Dvőrák and Berlioz had been introduced; Carl Formès had made his first English re-appearance for twenty years; and in 1889 Mendelssohn's *Elijah* was given on Festival scale with immediate and striking success before an audience of 24,000 persons.

The 1888-89 season saw many distinguished British productions at the Palace—Mackenzie's Overture to *Twelfth Night*, Parry's *Judith*, a Symphony by Stanford, Prout's Overture to *Rokeby*, and other works by McCunn, Bridge, Barnett, Cliffe, and Gadsby.

A further evidence of the affectionate gratitude felt towards Manns is afforded by the following letter of Thomas Wingham, a pupil of Sterndale Bennett, and for many years Director of the Music at the Brompton Oratory:—

Oxford Mansions,

April 13th, 1889

My dear Sir,

Again you have added to the many obliga-

Wingham's Gratefulness

tions I am under to you by the highly finished and
delicate performance of my piece[1] this afternoon.
I thought it a most admirable performance. The
cornet solo, clarinet solo, and little bit for the four
'cellos were all alike most beautifully rendered, as
was also *con sordini* accompaniment for violins.
And I must also thank you for your *great thought-
fulness* in playing my piece on the birthday of my
great master, thus reminding the public of my
musical relationship to him ; and how well the
orchestra played Sir Sterndale's masterly Overture.[2]
I never remember a finer performance ; I could not
help thinking what pleasure it would have given
dear Bennett could he have known (during the many
weary hours of teaching) that his birthday would
have been remembered and celebrated by such a
performance after his death. And this reminds me
to tell you how my own heavy labours are softened
and cheered by the knowledge that " something of
mine " is down for a Crystal Palace Concert. Often
has this thought lightened a whole term's teaching,

---

[1] Andante from Serenade in E flat.

[2] According to Crystal Palace Catalogue the Overture
by Bennett on that date was the *Naiads*.

August Manns

and I am grateful to you for it as only a professional man can be.

I am, dear Sir,

Most gratefully and sincerely yours,

THOMAS WINGHAM.

In the summer of 1888 Manns was induced by Sir George Grove to accompany him on his Continental holiday, and the following account of the trip, as told in Mr. Graves' *Life of Sir George Grove*, is mainly transcribed from the latter's diary.

Leaving London on the morning of August 7th with his friend, Mr. Manns, they crossed to Calais in lovely weather, the first stopping-place being Cologne (the scene of Manns' early successes thirty-eight years before). In the morning of the 8th the Conservatorium was visited, presumably by both the travellers, who went on to Frankfort in the afternoon. Here they called at Madame Schumann's, who was, unfortunately, away, and at midday on the 9th were on the road to Nuremberg, where they spent the night, reaching Bayreuth on the 10th. It is pretty evident that Manns had expressed

Abroad with Grove

admiration of *Meistersinger* and *Tristan*, for Grove writes home:—"I should probably agree with Manns about the *Meistersinger*, but as to *Tristan*, never! To it I have a distinct and strong moral objection, which with me will always strongly affect my judgment about Art." The two friends heard *Parsifal* also, with which Grove confesses himself "disappointed and very wearied."

At Bayreuth they parted, Grove going on for a longer tour to Vienna and Manns returning home.

In December 1888, Manns' attention was drawn to some not unfavourable criticism of a Saturday Concert, in the *Star* newspaper, and, as was occasionally his custom, he wrote to inquire the name and personality of the writer. His inquiry drew the following reply:—

> 29 FITZROY SQUARE, LONDON, W.,
>
> *December 19th*, 1888.
>
> DEAR SIR,
>
> Your right to know the name of the writer who ventures to criticize you in a public newspaper is unquestionable. He is, however, a person of no consequence whatever,—one who occasionally indulges himself with a Saturday trip to the Palace

August Manns

on the strength of being able to earn the price of his ticket (a considerable sum to him) by a stray notice in the *Star* or perhaps the *Pall Mall Gazette*. He has no position or reputation which entitle him to the smallest consideration as a writer on music. Musical critics, as you know, are of two sorts, musicians who are no writers and writers who are no musicians. The *Star* adventurer belongs to the second class, and he was never more astonished and flattered in his life than when he learned that his irresponsible sallies had attracted your attention. If his name were one to speak for itself, he would not intrude upon you with the explanations, but would simply enclose the card of one who is at least musical enough to feel deeply indebted to you and to sign himself,

Yours, most respectfully,

G. BERNARD SHAW.

AUGUST MANNS, Esq.

LIST OF THE ORCHESTRA, 1888-89.

First Violins.

Mr. C. Jung (principal)
  „ J. W. Breedon
  „ H. Celis
  „ V. Collins

Mr. W. H. Eayres
  „ C. J. Hayes
  „ O. Manns
  „ G. Müller
  „ A. W. Payne

Orchestra, 1888-89

First Violins.
Mr. E. Roberts
„ E. A. Rochester
„ V. Schmidt
„ W. Sutton
„ A. Verek

Second Violins.
Mr. A. Reynolds (prin.)
„ J. Earnshaw
„ E. Frewen
„ J. W. Gunniss
„ H. D. Haarnack
„ Hachenberger
„ H. Lewis
„ E. A. Lockwood
„ J. H. Novak
„ J. Spelman
„ G. Taylor
„ S. J. Waud
„ J. Weaver
„ J. B. Zerbini

Violas.
Mr. H. Krause (prin.)
„ E. Deane
„ C. W. Doyle
„ W. H. Hann
„ T. Lawrence
„ T. Reynolds
„ A. Stehling *
„ S. R. Webb
„ F. A. Wirth
„ A. Wright

'Cellos.
Mr. R. H. Reed (prin.)
„ J. Boatwright
„ J. Geary
„ H. P. Kleine
„ R. Melling
„ C. Ould
„ W. F. Reed *
„ H. Trust
„ E. Woolhouse

Contra Basso.
Mr. J. H. Waud
„ A. Collins
„ W. J. Griffiths
„ A. Cooke
„ N. Morel
„ E. Ould
„ W. A. Sutch
Mr. J. P. Waud
„ C. Winterbottom

Flutes.
Mr. A. Wells *
„ A. Tootill

Piccolo.
Mr. J. Wilcocke

Clarinets.
Mr. G. A. Clinton
„ G. T. Webb *

Bass Clarinet.
Mr. E. Augarde

* The names so marked were members of the original orchestra.

August Manns

Oboes.

Mr. W. M. Malsch

  ,, A. Peisel

Cor Anglais.

Mr. H. Smith

Bassoons.

Mr. W. Wotton

  ,, T. Wotton

Double Bassoon.

Mr. J. Hawes

Horns.

Mr. W. Naldrett

  ,, R. Keevill

  ,, C. Clinton

  ,, A. Stock

Cornets.

Mr. L. W. Hardy

  ,, S. West

Trumpets.

Mr. F. McGrath

  ,, P. W. Neuzerling

Trombones.

Mr. C. Hadfield

  ,, C. Geard

  ,, A. Phasey

Tuba.

Mr. J. H. Guilmartin

Tympani.

Mr. J. A. Smith

Side-Drum, Triangle.

Mr. C. Henderson

Bass Drum.

Mr. Wilmore

Harps.

Mr. E. Lockwood

  ,, E. Deane

Librarians.

Mr. S. West

A. Brennen

Organist—Mr. A. J. Eyre.

The opening weeks of the 1889-90 season were rich in novelties, Sullivan's music to *Macbeth* and Edward German's Overture to *Richard III.* among them; several great artistes appeared—Joachim, Sapellnikoff,—whose first Crystal Palace appearance this was,—Miss Fanny Davies, and others.

Handel's "Gloria Patri"

The following season Paderewski and Leonard Borwick each made their Crystal Palace *debût* within the same fortnight, both electing to be heard in Schumann's Pianoforte Concerto. Mr. German again appears in the programme, this time in a more ambitious work, a Symphony in E minor, which he conducted himself.

In the interval between this and the next (1891-92) season, came the fast-recurring Handel Festival, with the enormously increased labour and anxiety it entailed. This was the fourth of the series conducted by Manns, and it showed no diminution of power and finish on the part of conductor or performers. There was, however, a falling off to the extent of some 6000 in the audience over the four days, the only one which proved an exception being the ever-popular "Selection" Day, on which a novelty of great interest was performed in the *Gloria Patri*, composed in 1707, when Handel was a young man of twenty-three. The story of the MS. from which the copies were printed is remarkable. The piece itself is of unique interest, as being the only one Handel is known to have written for

August Manns

double orchestra and chorus. The original MS. was sold at Puttick & Simpson's in 1858 to Mr. Kerslake of Clifton, and was destroyed in a fire in 1860. Happily, a copy had been made, and this was bought by Dr. W. H. Cummings in 1878, and lent by him to the Handel Festival for the first performance.

Encouraged by the success of the *Elijah*, but a short time before, Manns produced *St. Paul* in June of this year on Festival scale, and with his usual success.

In the autumn programmes of 1891, many matters of great interest are to be found, for which brief reference must suffice. The first appearance of Popper the celebrated 'cello composer and player, a newly-published overture of Cherubini's, dating from 1815, the first appearance of Eugene Oudin at the Palace, and the playing by Joachim of the now celebrated Violin Concerto No. 3 of Max Bruch.

In June 1892, the performance of a composition by Mr. Barclay Jones (the present Director of the Music at the Brompton Oratory), brought a letter of warm thanks from his predecessor and

Sir August Manns conducting a Handel Festival.

Married Again

master, Thomas Wingham, who in regretting his enforced absence from the concert, bemoaned his fate in being "tied to the leg of a grand piano all my life."

In 1892-93, works by Dvǒrák, Mackenzie, Corder, and others were produced. The first-named had been richly represented at the Palace, his five Symphonies, two Concertos, and many other works, including the popular *Spectre's Bride*, all having had a hearing.

We must not omit to record that in August 1892, the first of several highly-prized royal honours was bestowed on Manns by his Majesty the German Emperor, William II., in the shape ot the Order of the Royal Crown, Fourth Class, on the occasion of his Majesty visiting the Crystal Palace with the Empress.

In January 1893, Manns became for the second time a widower, remaining so for four years, during which time his devoted daughter, Mrs. Fritz Bönten, resided with him in Harold Road, Upper Norwood, until his marriage on January 7th, 1897, with Miss Wilhelmina Thellusson, to whose gentle kindness and unselfish love that

August Manns

so greatly cheered the declining years of his life, he often referred in touching terms.

In the same month he received the following letter from his friend Dr. Mackenzie, to whom he had addressed a congratulatory note:—

15 Regent Park Road, N.W.,

January 3rd, 1893.

My dear old Friend,

Nobody could have been more surprised than I was to receive the letters of honour on Monday last. Your kind words are like yourself, and with that I say nearly all. Not quite. We English musicians owe you a great debt. I owe you many, for you have ever been kind and generous to me, from my first start as a suckling composer.

Take these few words as they are meant, in sincere acknowledgment of your good-will to me at all times.

With my wife's best wishes for your own health— which means the happiness of all around you.

Believe me,

Very faithfully yours,

A. Manns, Esq.   A. C. MACKENZIE.

'94 Handel Festival

During the 1893-94 season the death of Gounod occurred, and was duly commemorated by the performance of a selection from his works. Wagner appears to hold a prominent place in the season's work, with music by Villiers Stanford and Bantock, among British composers; Paderewski and Lady Hallé lending the distinction of their appearance among the soloists of the season.

Nothing is more curious in Manns' character than the almost pathetic eagerness with which he welcomed newspaper criticism when, *bien entendu*, it was favourable; or his despondency if, perchance, it was the reverse. In 1893 he writes to Bennett that "the very kind comments in the *Daily Telegraph* have given me new blood for new exertions on behalf of good music. I have been perfectly hungering for lines of this kind from you, and therefore cannot refrain from telling you, in my own undisguised way, that you have made me happy."

In 1894, the fifth Handel Festival under Manns' conductorship took place, and while little can be said that is new of these triennial performances, it must be insisted that each

August Manns

Festival that passes renders the selection of pieces for its successor a matter of the greatest anxiety to the conductor. There are, of course, the *Messiah* and *Israel in Egypt* (always the two *pièces de résistance* for the second and fourth days), but the demand of the public and the critics for novelty on Selection Day cannot be disregarded without outcry. The first day, that devoted to the rehearsal, was, we may here remark, not only so in name, but under Manns was always in very truth a real rehearsal. Under Sir Michael Costa it was not so to the same extent. He would go through with perhaps one or two stoppages for correction, but with Manns things were different. A noted critic remarks upon the rehearsal day in this very year that for Manns the audience might have been non-existent. "Mr. Manns arrested the march of his army when he pleased, and chose to do so very often, teaching alike by example and precept what should be done, occasionally to the amusement of the public, always to the advantage of the music." An unusual incident is recorded during the performance of *Israel in Egypt*, which can

Joseph Bennett

be paralleled by a similar occurrence many
years before under Costa. This was nothing less
than a false start in the chorus, "And with
the blast of Thy nostrils," necessitating a fresh
commencement of the number. The year is
further memorable for the first appearance of
Miss Clara Butt as the contralto, and of Mr.
Walter Hedgcock (the present director of the
Palace music), as the organist at the Festival.
The attendance of the public, however, showed a
further falling off of some 4000 in comparison
with the previous occasion, although the critics
held it to have been artistically the most
successful since the series began in 1857.

The following letter was addressed to Mr.
Joseph Bennett by Manns a few days after
the Festival of 1894. Rightly does its recipient
point out how "a mere musician" may endure
suffering as a hero, in the pursuit of his gentle
art :—

"As a subscriber to and constant reader of the
Daily Telegraph, I, of course, saw your censure
on the shortcomings of the reproduction of two

August Manns

of the choruses in the second part of *Israel in Egypt*. Please do not be angry with my endeavour to acquaint you with the chief cause of these short-comings. I have struggled since last December to combat and cure rheumatism in both shoulders, and although I had succeeded so far that I could get through my conductor's labours in Glasgow, and afterwards here at my orchestral concerts, my enemy would not leave me. I had to go through the six preliminary piano (chorus) rehearsals as best I could, and the result was this—when in the midst of the chorus 'Wretched Lovers' last Wednesday, my right shoulder cracked as if its bones were crushed. The hitherto smouldering pain became of a sudden very acute. I tried my best with nursing during Wednesday night and Thursday, but had to approach my work on Friday with a foreboding of trouble. The trouble came. I could not lift my conducting arm sufficiently high, nor could I give the beat that accentuated swing without which the 3,600 performers cannot be kept together. The beat at the beginning of the two choruses in question having to be done with the fore-arm, was not distinct enough for the far-off choristers—hence the failure."

Naturalized

It must not be omitted that on May 21st, 1894, Manns, already by adoption and habit a Briton, took out letters of naturalization as a British subject, almost exactly forty years after his first arrival in this country.

In October 1895, a remarkable concert took place at the Palace, restricted to works by British composers who had made their first appearance at the Saturday Concerts under the ægis of the venerated conductor. Among the composers so honoured were Sullivan, Parry, Mackenzie, and Stanford, a quartette of British musicians whose names alone justify, if justification were needed, the policy of steadily encouraging our composers.

During the 1894-95 season a young English student of the Royal College of Music, Richard H. Walthew, who had also obtained some earlier teaching at the Guildhall School of Music, had a Choral Ballad, "The Pied Piper of Hamelin," accepted for performance at a Saturday Concert. Mr. Walthew kindly sends me the following sympathetic reference to his reception by Manns:—

August Manns

" His manner to me was not that of a master to a novice, but of one musician to another, which, of course, was very flattering to the young student. He was perfectly natural, and paid no unmeaning compliments. He suggested certain alterations in the score, and pointed out many passages which he considered unnecessarily difficult; and he was quite right, although I did not think so at the time. He studied the work with the greatest care (and I have always thought it strange that any one not an Englishman should have entered so completely into the idiomatic humour of Browning's poem), and blue-pencilled the score all through with nuances, etc., that I had omitted to indicate. Moreover, he was the only conductor I have ever met who got my *tempi* right the very first time. It seemed a kind of instinct. . . . I occasionally came across him afterwards at the Palace, and was always greeted with a bar or two of the Piper's little tune !

" Manns left ðn my mind an impression of great personal dignity without a suspicion of pose, combined with real friendliness and good nature, and I am glad to pay my humble tribute to his memory."

CHAPTER VI.

THE 12th March 1895 was the seventieth birth-day of August Manns, an occasion which, it was felt by his friends and admirers, ought not to be allowed to pass without some special mark of their affection and veneration. From his old colleague, Grove, he received the following letter:—

March 11th, 1895.

MY DEAR MANNS,

I send you my sincere and affectionate wishes for a good and happy anniversary for your birthday to-morrow.

There will be many in England who will wish it to you, but none who has more reason to do so than I, your old friend of just forty years' standing.

August Manns

They say that no one can know a man really till he has done business with him and travelled with him. We have done both, and my judgment is that in both our affection has been cemented. It is now a good solid block, and so may it remain till it pleases a good Providence to dissolve it by death!

That you may see many a future anniversary of to-morrow is, my dear old friend, the prayer of

Yours very affectionately,

G. GROVE.

My wife asks me to send you her very kindest remembrances.

It may be well here to devote a few lines to the relations that existed between these two strong men over such a strenuous and lengthy period of their lives. The writer has had the privilege of consulting some who knew them both intimately, and who have referred to a time when Manns may have felt perhaps a certain soreness, almost amounting to resentment, that his own share in the revolution in musical taste that had been effected by the Saturday Concerts was not better appreciated by the public. It was probably intensified by the fact that the official

A Rift

honours which at length fell to Manns were delayed until the evening of his career, and long after, not only the musical world, but the public at large, had felt that such rewards were rightly due.[1] But it was almost inevitable that Grove, with his almost feverish earnestness and his genius for inspiring others with enthusiasm, should unconsciously leave the impression in the minds of those even who were well aware of Manns' true value that he was the mainspring of the whole affair. Needless to say that it was not of set purpose—nay, more, that it would have distressed Grove infinitely to think that he (Grove) was detracting from the other's just dues. He was eager at all times that they

---

[1] It is but fair to state, however, that Manns had himself many years before refused to accede to the suggestion made by Grove and other of his friends that application should be made in the proper quarters for the knighthood he eventually received. His motive for this refusal was the feeling that jealousy might be created at an honour given to a foreigner when such dignities were not quite so freely bestowed upon musicians as was the case in later years.

should be recognized and properly appraised. Mr. Graves says:—

" He was fully conscious of these [his musical] limitations, and never made the slightest pretence to any knowledge that he did not possess; and when occasion demanded, invariably had recourse to experts to supply his deficiencies—to Mr. Manns or Mr. Dannreuther, Mr. C. A. Barry or Dr. Charles Wood."

He (Grove) was even embarrassed by the public reference to his labours at the testimonial given to him in 1880. "Laying it on too thickly and (as it happened) unjustly with regard to two people in the room," are his own words. It is perhaps not straining the point too far to surmise that one of the two was Manns. Then his auto-biographical speech, quoted earlier in this work, if nothing else existed, would serve to clear his memory of any suspicion that he "stole his thunder" from other people. That he had exceptional powers of assimilating information was undoubted, but not his worst enemy could have justly charged him with parading it as his own.

Mr. Bennett, in his recently-published *Forty*

Healing the Wound

Years of Music, prints the following letter from Sir George Grove, written to himself in 1876 in reference to the subject:—

" I want to ask a kindness from you. Manns is in a terrible state of grief owing to various remarks in the papers recently, which seem to give me more credit than is due—or rather to give him less—in reference to the Saturday Concerts. He urges that I am spoken of as if the choice of the programmes and the excellence of the execution and the entire success of the concerts were due to me. I can't see the inference, but he does and is terribly hurt and distressed. He is over-sensitive; but, on the other hand, he is so able and devoted, and has done so much more for music than any conductor that I have had to do with in England, that I should be very glad if he could be relieved in some way. He urges me to write to the papers, but this I am determined not to do. But it occurs to me that you could easily say something in your next notice that would heal the wound, and I am sure you will be glad to do so both for my sake and his. I have written in the same sense to Ryan and J. W. D."

August Manns

Bennett tentatively attributes the misunderstanding on the part of the public to its obvious cause—"the prominence of Grove as the literary mouthpiece of the concerts." Grove's letter continues:—

" The merits of Manns as conductor and musician have been discussed not only at large, but also with rare oneness of feeling and unanimity of opinion. In this his memory will evermore be happy; and on the strength of unqualified acclaim his adopted land will, let us all hope, preserve to him 'a broad approach to fame.' It was impossible to watch Manns in the act of conducting without being assured he was supersensitive and in popular language 'a bundle of nerves.' Inordinately endowed with this quality, so necessary to a musician and so often a heavy cross to be borne, it is not surprising that Manns deeply felt adverse criticism, when it was purely the honest and moderate expression of an opinion."

To revert in this connection to the Manns birthday celebration, Grove's speech to his old friend upon presenting him with the testimonial may be appropriately quoted:—

Birthday Celebration

"The friends and admirers whom you see around you on this happy occasion have assembled for more than one purpose. First, we desire to congratulate you on the attainment of a term of years which musicians are not very often permitted to reach. Secondly, we wish to express our pleasure at your happy recovery from your recent severe illness. Thirdly, we have to express our gratitude for your efforts at the head of the Crystal Palace Orchestra, by which the works of many of the great composers have been introduced to England by your means in a manner well worthy of the fame of those great men. Fourthly,—and this is a matter which rouses not only our artistic sentiments, but the deep feelings of our hearts,—we desire to express to you our warm thanks for the singularly happy position which you have taken and maintained since your advent among us with regard to English musicians. Foreigner as you are by birth, no Englishman could have given more encouragement to our native school than you have given by your cordial behaviour to a multitude of our composers and performers, by the extraordinary pains you have bestowed upon their works, and the careful and brilliant performances by which you have in many cases introduced

August Manns

them to the public. Such benefits as these can never fade from the memory, and we here try to tender you our heartfelt thanks for them, and our earnest hope that your beneficent and useful career may be still prolonged for many years.

"As your first friend in this country, I may be permitted to acknowledge before this distinguished assembly the honour and gratification which I have felt at working by your side for many years in the realization of your splendid design and the pleasure which our uninterrupted friendship has given me."

The movement to commemorate the anniversary had fittingly originated with the premier musical association of Great Britain, the Philharmonic Society, at a general meeting held on the 2nd February 1895 (Dr. W. H. Cummings in the chair). On the proposition of Sir A. C. Mackenzie, seconded by Mr. Charles Bannister, it was resolved "to commemorate the seventieth birthday of Mr. August Manns, his loyal encouragement of British music, and his general devotion to the highest forms of musical art, by inviting him to a reception at an early date."

The movement grew apace; a committee was

A Demonstration

formed which included every one in **England** with any claim to the title of musician, together with many other eminent men whose names are household words wherever the English language is spoken.

Great as the former demonstration of affection and respect had been, this one far surpassed it. Many of those who had formerly testified by their support to the gratitude all Englishmen felt to August Manns were now, alas! gone over to the majority; but all those who remained, with many others added to them, united in paying homage to their venerated friend. The reception took place at the Grafton Galleries, Bond Street, on Tuesday, April 30th, and was attended by an extraordinary gathering of celebrities, headed by H.R.H. the Duke of Saxe-Coburg and Gotha, who conferred upon Manns the Order of Kunst and Wissenschaft (Science and Art).

It should certainly be placed upon record who were those distinguished persons in music, art, and science that, in honouring August Manns by their presence on the great occasion, no less certainly did honour to themselves. They were as follows:—

August Manns

Lord Chelmsford, G.C.B., Sir Algernon Borth-
wick, Bart., M.P. (afterwards Lord Glenesk), Sir
George Grove, C.B., Sir Arthur Sullivan, Sir
Joseph Barnby, Sir Alexander C. Mackenzie, Sir
Augustus Harris, Sir Walter Parratt, Sir Frederick
Abel, the President of the Royal Society and
Lady Kelvin, Sir John Puleston, Archdeacon
Sinclair, Sir Richard Webster (now Lord Chief
Justice of England), Judge Meadows White, Sir
Hubert Parry, Sir J. Frederick Bridge, Sir C.
Villiers Stanford, Professor Ebenezer Prout, Pro-
fessor Hubert Herkomer, R.A., Alfred Gilbert,
R.A., David Murray, R.A., J. McWhirter, R.A.,
Herr Wilhelmj, Madam Albani, J. F. Barnett,
Oscar Barrett, C. A. Barry, Clara Butt, Francesco
Beringer, Oscar Beringer, Henry Bird, Leonard
Borwick, Lennox Brown, Andrew Black, David
Bispham, J. T. Carrodus, Dr. W. H. Cummings,
J. Spencer Curwen, Alfred Caldicott, Anderson
Critchett, Fanny Davies, Edward Dannreuther,
Mary Davies, Signor Denza, Eaton Faning,
Barrington Foote, B. L. Farjeon, Mme. Fricken-
haus, Madame Hope Glenn, Mrs. Goetz, Edward
German, Manuel Garcia, Otto Goldschmidt,

A Rally of Friends

Wilhelm Ganz, G. Henschel, A. J. Hipkins, Fritz Hartvigson, Dr. Joachim, Mme. Janotha, Agnes Janson, William Kuhe, Edward Lloyd, Alfred Littleton, Stanley Lucas, Walter Macfarren, Hamish McCunn, Marian McKenzie, Mary Moore, Daniel Mayer, M. Maybrick, Tivadar Nachez, Esther Palliser, Alberto Randegger, Mrs. Ronalds, Mrs. Carl Rosa, C. Santley, Émile Sauret, B. Schonberger, Felix Semon, W. Shakespeare, Mme. Lemmens Sherrington, Leo Schuster, Solomon J. Solomon, Norman Salmond, Clara Samuell, Franklin Taylor, John Thomas, Signor Tosti, A. J. R. Trendell, C.M.G., Thomas Threlfall, Miss Thudichum, Hope Temple, Helen Trust, E. H. Turpin, N. Vert, Albert Visetti, Anna Williams, Hilda Wilson, Sir Charles Wyndham, Agnes Zimmerman, and the Hon. Sec., Hermann Klein.

The members of the Crystal Palace Orchestra had gracefully volunteered their services for the occasion, and a selection of pieces by the musicians to whom Manns had done such good service was played. Sir George Grove—amongst those present, certainly his oldest friend—read the formal address,

August Manns

and supplemented it by the generous and cordial speech to which reference has already been made. The presentation took the form of an illuminated album, in which the signatures of those supporting the reception appeared.

In a note by Manns himself concerning this, one of the red-letter days of his life, he says—"The most gratifying contribution to this reception for me consisted of the following lines from Mr. Joseph Bennett, the musical critic of the *Daily Telegraph*, inscribed in the Reception Programme:—

"Honour to the man who, by industry and perseverance, making right use of his talents, wins the highest place, and fills it with the modest dignity which disarms even envy.

"Honour to the musician who serves his Art with a single eye to its greater glory; who has learned to keep lesser aims in subjection, whose thorough devotion shrinks from no sacrifice of self.

"Honour to the conductor who, rising above prejudice and limiting influences, recognizes every form of musical good; whose sympathies are as wide as his Art; who labours with equal zeal on

Acknowledgment

behalf of whatever things therein are lovely and of good report.

"Honour especially be his to whom it may in truth be said:

> 'The secret consciousness
> Of duty well performed: the public voice
> Of praise that honours virtue, and rewards it,
> All these are yours.'

"Honour, therefore, to AUGUST MANNS."

It is not necessary to present our readers with the full text of the lengthy address which Sir George Grove read to its honoured recipient, but the speech the latter made in reply, with its pathetic little reference to the "snow-clad old man," its humorous description of the "chaff" he endured when that snowy hair was raven-black, is thoroughly characteristic of the man and is here given in full:—

"Your Royal Highness, my Lords, and Ladies and Gentlemen, I thank you, Gentlemen of the Committee, most sincerely for the flattering terms in which you have referred to my work at the Crystal

August Manns

Palace in the Address which has just been read by
my valued friend, Sir George Grove; and you,
Ladies and Gentlemen, I thank equally heartily for
your very cordial sympathy with these, for me, more
than complimentary comments.

"I feel deeply grateful for the honour you are thus
conferring upon me, because I am thereby assured
once more that my art-work amongst you during
now nearly forty years has been understood and
appreciated.

"I say 'nearly forty years,' but, as a matter of
fact, it was this day forty-one years ago when I
arrived in England and entered the service of the
Crystal Palace Company as Sub-Conductor, and this
day forty years when I received the offer of the
Conductorship from the Directors of the Crystal
Palace through Sir George Grove.

"Let me assure you that it will remain a special
source of happiness for me to know that I have not
only been able to conduct Concerts during these
many years which have so largely helped to promote
the progress of musical art in Great Britain, but that
I have also succeeded in conducting myself in a
manner which has gained me the approbation of the
various classes of patrons of good music, and also

"These Forty Years"

the esteem, and in some cases the affection, of my professional brethren and sisters; a prize which I consider to be the highest and most valuable that can be gained by any honest-working conductor of music.

"How this prize was won is known to a good many of you, and I need therefore not weary you by self-biographical details about the progress of that art-work which has been accomplished under my guidance during the forty years of my connection with the Crystal Palace.

"That these forty years have not passed without a good deal of trouble and anxiety needs no affirmation. It had to be proved that good music had more chance to find its way to the hearts of the people than bad or indifferent music; that was not an easy task to accomplish, because the distrust in what is called 'classical music' was, at the beginning of my career, very formidable. All troubles were, however, gradually overcome with the help of my friend, Sir George Grove, and with the help of the Press, and more particularly by that of the then musical critic of *The Times*, the late Mr. J. W. Davison, who let no opportunity pass for pointing to the great benefit which the Crystal Palace Concerts were capable of producing on behalf

August Manns

of the then much desired nursing of musical art amongst the people.

" There was another source of trouble in store for me, which, however, I had brought upon myself by that tremendous crop of long black hair which I so lovingly cultivated at that time; week after week did the postman bring me big letters with curl papers of every description, enclosing always neatly written advice how to use them, and tiny pink letters with enclosures of threepenny bits, with the request to go to a barber and have my hair cut.

" These delightful communications came, as I found out afterwards, from some of the young ladies' schools at Norwood and Sydenham; but I never found out whether these young ladies teased me because they loved me, or whether they had a less pleasant motive for their amusing attention. Should by any chance some of these ladies be in this room at this moment, they might now relieve me of all further uncertainty in this matter by making a clean breast of it. I assure them honestly that I have forgiven them long ago.

" These expositions of my troubles at the earliest stages of my labours at the Crystal Palace have led me up to 'The Ladies!' Ah, the ladies! That is

" The Ladies "

a grand motto for a speech of a musician! I believe myself to be fairly correct when saying that none of the arts are more indebted to the patronage of the ladies than ours. Where would the recitalists be without the ladies? Where would the principal tenori and bassi-cantanti of the opera and concert-room be without the ladies? Where would that snow-clad old man, who is now talking to you, have been with the work he had to do at the Crystal Palace during the whole of the summer and autumn of his life without the constant attention of the ladies? It was the gentle patter of their little feet and tiny hands wherewith they received and encouraged him when stepping up to the platform, and wherewith they always rewarded his efforts to please them during the performances, and where-with they kept up his sometimes flagging spirits and gave him new blood for new exertions.

" Gentlemen of the Executive Committee, among the many items in your arrangements for this evening, for which I am specially indebted to you, is your happy thought of providing me with an opportunity of thoroughly facing the ladies after having been compelled to turn my back on them for so many years. I now can thank them for all the

August Manns

delights which their gentle patronage has brought me, and assure them that the promptings of my heart about them are in the sweetest of sweet concord with the immortal Scotch poet, Robert Burns, when he sings:

> 'There's naught but care on every han',
>> In ev'ry hour that passes;
> What signifies the life o' man
> An' 'twere na for the lasses!'

Ladies! I do thank you with all my heart for having honoured me by gracing this reception with your presence.

"Having just referred to my having now spent the whole of the summer and autumn of my life, I am brought face to face with the stern fact that I have now entered the list of old men with only life's winter before me. What that winter will bring me none can know. But we all know that, as an English poet has very charmingly expressed it,

> 'As sure as autumn has its flowers
> Blue skies will cheer our wintry hours.'

The colour of blue is, I think, emblematical of constancy. It will require no assurance on my part that I shall remain constant in the principles of my

Music's Influence

liberal music creed so long as Providence enables me to beat time—that is, to produce Concerts at the Crystal Palace which will, at least approachingly, realize the aims of those gentlemen who established this unique resort for elevating pleasure nearly half a century ago.

"Yes, I shall always endeavour to provide musical entertainments which shall combine elevating amusement with instruction for all who may listen to them; for I am a thorough believer in the views which Milton expresses in his *Tractate on Education,* namely, that

'Music, if wise men and prophets be not extremely out, has a great power over dispositions and manners, to smooth and make them gentle from rustic harshness and distemper'd passions.'

"Having now taxed your patience rather severely with these various quotations, I will only add one more, and, moreover, one which will bring you comfort—namely, it is recorded that Queen Elizabeth, when one day having to receive a somewhat unwelcome deputation, addressed that deputation, by way of prelude, in the following words:—

'Gentlemen! Please remember that speeches we like best when they are over.'

August Manns

I, knowing that all of you agree with Queen Elizabeth's views about speeches, will now only thank you once more earnestly and sincerely for the great honour you have done me by your presence at this reception; an honour which will remain engraved on my heart until the last moments of my life, and will subsequently be lovingly cherished by those who have a special interest in my welfare—namely, my daughter and granddaughter.

" Once more, Ladies and Gentlemen, thanks, thanks, sincerely warm-hearted thanks to all of you for that esteem and affection wherewith you have rewarded my humble efforts as a conductor of music."

The Grafton Gallery reception by no means exhausts the messages of felicitation from all sides which April 1895 saw heaped upon Manns. Irving sent him "love and greetings"; Sims Reeves wrote, "All loving wishes for the future. . . . Ever your sincere old friend."

The kindly wishes were, if possible, intensified by some anxiety that had been felt earlier in the year for his health, an attack of bronchitis having caused a rare—indeed, for him, almost unique—temporary absence from duty.

Strange Fact

There had been in January, also, of this great year of his life a large gathering in Glasgow at a complimentary banquet, "in recognition of his eminent services to the cause of music in Glasgow," on which occasion a gold-mounted ivory bâton was presented by the chairman, General Sir Donald Matheson, who, in thanking (*see ante*, p. 121) him for his fifteen years' services to the Choral and Orchestral Society, offered him a hearty welcome "in that blessed hour when we shall meet thee again."

In April 1895, there was printed at the Crystal Palace a catalogue of the principal instrumental and choral works performed at the Saturday Concerts from October 1855 to May 1895. In the preface to this pamphlet, contributed by Manns, he mentions the curious fact "that amongst the frequent applications for the loan of scores and parts of various unusual works which have from time to time been performed at the Crystal Palace Saturday Concerts, is one from Vienna itself—for one of Schubert's MS. Symphonies; a strange fact, upon which all who have co-operated in the establishment and

August Manns

healthy development of these concerts—*i.e.*, the directors, executants, critics and audience, and, more particularly, Sir George Grove—may look with special gratification."

There follows the preface a table of general statistics, from which we quote the following:—

Total No. of Compositions performed .	.	1550
,, ,, Symphonies, Suites, etc. .	.	195
,, ,, Overtures, Marches, Entr'actes, and detached Orchestral works		585
Concertos, Fantasias, etc. .	. .	576
Oratorios, Masses, Cantatas, and other Choral works		194
Number of Composers	.	300
German	.	104
English	.	82
French	.	39
Italian	.	26

The rest (49), Belgian, Bohemian, Danish, Dutch, Hungarian, Polish, Russian, Spanish, and Swedish.

These inspiring celebrations over, there still remained in Manns plenty of energy for work, and he returned with zest to his labours. A

South Wales Festival

long list of new works was heard in the 1894-95 season, among them Mackenzie's popular *Britannia* overture; a Te Deum for Orchestra and Organ, by Sgambati; a Violin Concerto of Moszkowski; Parry's Overture to *Job;* and other works by German, D'Albert, Goldmark, Arnott, and Walthew.

During the 1896-97 season there were an Overture, *Othello*, by Walter Macfarren, an old friend of Manns; a Suite by Madame Chaminade; and a Symphony by Barclay Jones, brought to Manns' notice by the enthusiastic recommendation of Grove.

At the end of the season rumours had been current that the famous series of concerts would not last another season, but Manns was able to announce at his benefit concert in April that, in spite of the lukewarm support they were receiving from the public, the directors would continue their enterprise.

In June 1896, Manns was induced to assume the conductorship of a new combination organized at Cardiff, under the title of the South Wales Musical Festival. The veteran conductor met

August Manns

with an enthusiastic welcome, and found a congenial task in guiding the music-loving Welsh choirs to success. Nor was his gluttony for hard work exhausted by this, for in the autumn the musical world learned that the Committee of the new Sheffield Festival had invited August Manns to bring his unrivalled experience and prestige to give their enterprise a good send-off.

In October, therefore, we find him at the Cutlers' Hall, Sheffield, the guest of honour for the evening of the Duke of Norfolk, then Mayor of Sheffield. On the morrow he had the familiar task of piloting a huge orchestra and chorus through *Elijah*, with his old friend Santley at his elbow to sustain with his unparalleled art the title-rôle of the great prophet, as he only, since the oratorio was first written, has been able to sustain it. Later in the week the superb voices of the Sheffield choir, who owed so much to Dr. Coward's training, as Manns gladly acknowledged, were heard in the *Golden Legend* and *Job*.

It was no slight physical feat for a man of

" Thus spake Zarathustra "

seventy-one years to journey 170 miles to the great Yorkshire city on a Monday morning, attend a big banquet, after rehearsal, in the evening; conduct *Elijah* in the Albert Hall, Sheffield, on Tuesday morning, and the *Golden Legend* in the afternoon, attend another reception in the evening; conduct *Job* on the Wednesday morning, and Berlioz's *Faust* in the evening, and return home, to use a colloquialism, " as fresh as paint."

The 1896-97 season included, besides many other novelties, the Tone-poem of Richard Strauss, "Thus spake Zarathustra," which brought the following letter from the composer :—

[TRANSLATION].

MUNICH,

March 16*th*, 1897.

VERY HONOURED COLLEAGUE,

I heard from Mr. Spitzweg, and also saw in the London newspapers, that the same sympathetic interest which you gave last year to my " Till Eulenspiegel " you have now again given to my new Tone-poem, " Also sprach Zarathustra," and

August Manns

that you brought its first performance about with personal sacrifice and by means of your transcendent skill secured for the piece a splendid performance.

Please receive for this the assurance of my sincere gratitude and admiration, to which I add the warm wish that I may soon be able to make your acquaintance and thank you personally. Accept, most honoured sir, my most cordial greetings and the expression of my especial esteem, with which I remain,

Your sincerely devoted

RICHARD STRAUSS.

1897 brought with it the customary triennial Festival, the sixth that had been held under the bâton of Manns. It had been feared that the imminent nearness of the Diamond Jubilee celebrations might tend to diminish the numbers of the audience, but if this was the case, it was barely noticeable. One of the great critics had observed faults at rehearsal of which he freely admitted the absence at the performance, while qualifying his praise with the reservation that neither chorus nor instrumentalists " touched the highest mark of these festivals."

British Compositions

In 1897, 1898, and 1899 a very large number of compositions by British musicians was heard at the Palace, as though the veteran conductor, with but a short space of time remaining to him—for it was known that the great series of Saturday Concerts was nearing its end—was determined to show his staunch friendship right to the last. The list included a Symphonic Poem, *Hamlet* (German); Three Dances, "From the Bavarian Highlands" (Elgar); Symphonic Sketch, "Le Mer" (Gilson); Symphonic Prologue to Chaucer's *Canterbury Tales* (W. H. Bell).

The 1898-99 novelties were Fantasia on March Themes (German); Fantasia for Trumpet and Organ (Couldery); Ballade for Orchestra (Coleridge-Taylor); "Nachtlied" (Schumann); Variations Symphoniques for Violoncello and Orchestra (Boëllmann); Symphonic Prelude, "Kit Marlowe" (Herbert Bedford); Scena, "The Dream of Endymion" (Cowen); Symphonic Poem, "Sister Helen" (W. Wallace); Symphony No. 3 in D (Tschaïkowsky); Symphonic Poem, "The Pardoner's Tale" (W. H. Bell); Ballad for Baritone Solo, Chorus, and Orchestra,

August Manns

"Young Lochinvar" (Liza Lehmann); Choral Ballad, "Phaudrig Crohoore" (Stanford); Pianoforte Concerto No. 3 (Scharwenka); Orchestral Suite No. 2 in E (Reginald Steggall); Symphonic Poem, "Heldenlied" (Dvŏrák); Scène Espagnole Sevillaño (Elgar); and Valse Fantasia for Flute and Orchestra (Dunhill).

In 1899 there fell due the second Sheffield Festival, and again the charge of it was entrusted to Manns. The first had set such a high standard of extraordinary excellence that great pains had to be taken by all concerned to prove it had been no "flash in the pan," but the inevitable result of superlatively good voices well trained, continuous practice under highly capable conductors, and an enthusiasm that only those who know Yorkshire folk well can understand. Even Manns himself, long accustomed to the immense volume of tone at the Palace and elsewhere, declared he had never heard anything like it in his life. The orchestra was imported from the "Old Guard" at the Palace, and seven great orchestral and choral works were performed in the three days of which the festival consisted.

Second Sheffield Festival

Whether the hand of August Manns was responsible for the fact that three of the seven works were by English composers we know not, but the statement is at least suggestive of his influence.

At the Crystal Palace a Centenary Festival performance of Haydn's *Creation* was also given.

CHAPTER VII.

Reasons for the decline of popularity of Saturday Concerts—Manns' last Handel Festival, 1900—The new Amateur Orchestra at the Palace—Five orchestral concerts under Manns in 1901—Mr. Joseph Holbrooke's reminiscences of Manns—Dr. Cowen succeeds as Handel Festival conductor—Manns made a Doctor of Music of Oxford University—Presentations from Festival Choir—Manns receives honour of knighthood—More congratulations—Letters from prominent musicians—Speech at Whitefriars' Club—Manns' last concert, 11th June 1904 —Illness and death.

WITH the closing of the nineteenth century, as illustrious in music as in all that makes for the more material comfort and well-being of humanity, the long series of Saturday Concerts on the old scale also came to an end. At the time of its formal disbandment the *personnel* of the Crystal Palace Saturday Orchestra was as follows:—

THE FORTY-FOURTH ANNUAL SERIES OF
THE CRYSTAL PALACE
SATURDAY CONCERTS.
1899-1900.
CONDUCTOR—MR. AUGUST MANNS.

Orchestra, 1899-1900

First Violins.

Mr. A. V. Belinski (principal)
,, C. J. Aves
,, J. W. Breeden*
,, T. Carrington
,, V. Fawcett
,, R. Gray
,, C. J. Hayes*
,, H. Lewis*
,, O. Manns*
,, E. Messais
,, J. E. Platt
,, G. Schmidt
,, W. Sutton*
,, E. Wheldon

Second Violins.

Mr. H. Renard (principal)
,, De Beriot Green
,, J. Earnshaw*
,, A. Fossati
,, J. W. Gunnis*
,, H. D. Haarnack*
,, F. Hachenberger*
,, J. E. Hall
,, T. A. Kelley
,, W. B. Norris
,, J. Ricketts
,, S. J. Waud*

Violas.

Mr. O. Manns, jun. (principal)
,, J. Cruft
,, E. Deane*
,, M. Dolovitch

Mr. H. Krause
,, T. Lawrence*
,, K. A. Stehling*
,, F. A. Wirth*
,, A. Wright*
Another

Violoncellos.

Mr. M. Belinski (principal
,, J. Boatwright*
,, W. J. Claxton
,, R. Melling*
,, L. Paggi
,, C. N. Price
Mr. R. H. Reed
,, H. Trust*
,, E. Woolhouse

Double Basses.

Mr. W. H. Stewart (principal)
,, A. Collins*
,, A. Cooke*
,, W. Griffiths
,, N. Morel*
,, C. Stewart
,, W. R. Streather
,, W. A. Satch*
,, J. P. Waud*

Harps.

Mr. H. Fernbacher (principal)
,, E. Deane*

Flutes.

Mr. E. R. Hudson (principal)
,, F. Seidel
,, J. Hayes

August Manns

Piccolo.
Mr. J. Hayes

Oboes.
Mr. A. Robert (principal)
,, A. Hullaert
,, F. Montara

Cor Anglais.
Mr. E. Dubrucq

Clarinets
Mr. C. Fawcett (principal)
,, W. F. Gregory
,, H. G. Chapman

D Clarinet.
Mr J. Egerton

Bass Clarinet.
Mr. J. Park

Bassoons.
Mr. J. Anderson (principal)
,, E. Dubrucq
,, G. A. Day

Contra Fagotto.
Mr. W. Davis

Horns.
Mr. C. Clinton (principal)*
,, R. Spencer

Mr. L. Carvelli
,, J. Colton

Cornets.
Mr. L. W. Hardy (principal)*
,, J. C. Scotts

Trumpets.
Mr. W. Morrow (principal)
,, J. Solomon

Trombones.
Mr. F. K. Klink (alto)
,, H. Fawcett (tenor)
,, M. May (bass)

Bass Tuba.
Mr. F. McConnell

Timpani.
Mr. J. A. Smith*

Side Drum, Triangle, etc.
Mr. J. Farren
,, A. White

Glockenspiel.
Mr. J. Schroeder

Brass Drum, Cymbals, etc.
Mr. A. Smith

Organist and Accompanist—Mr. WALTER W. HEDGCOCK.
* The names so marked will be found in the band list of 1888-89.

True to the last to the advancement of
British art, Manns brought forward Elgar's
"Sea Pictures" and W. H. Bell's "Symphony

192

Orchestra Disbanded

in E major," among much other beautiful music.
In April 1900, the daily orchestra, which formed
the nucleus of the Saturday Concerts and great
festivals, was disbanded, to the great regret, no
doubt, of many, but in pursuance of a policy for
which it would be impossible to blame the Crystal
Palace directorate. It had long been known that
without more support from the public the inevitable end would be hastened, and some credit
is due to the Company for their obvious reluct-
ance to accept the verdict so unmistakably given
by the arbiters of the fate of all forms of public
entertainment. It was not necessary to look far
afield for the cause of the decline in popularity
of the Saturday Concerts. When the Palace was
built, and for many years after, it was unique.
It was possible, for a shilling or two, not only to
hear good music, but to see great works of art
and industry, to study a thousand objects of
interest, to enjoy a glorious landscape and lovely
gardens, and even to have a meal amidst
surroundings more closely approximating to the
fascinating Continental resorts than anything
Britishers had as yet experienced.

August Manns

Setting aside the fact that there were in 1900 other places in London itself where first-class music could be heard, all the attractions enumerated had become commonplace to the *blasé* Londoner. He could, if he lived in North London, see a fine view from the Alexandra Palace, he could pick and choose his art collection or gallery from a dozen which offered themselves, and finally he had the perennial Earl's Court Exhibitions in his very midst, each succeeding year striving to tempt his palate by more or less blatant advertisement of novel attractions. Besides all this, the Palace audiences, educated up to a high standard by Manns and the accomplished musicians whom he directed, had even in a measure been their own undoing, for they had formed a leaven which had spread the knowledge and appreciation of fine music far and wide over the great province of London and the home counties. It had been shown that there was a public ready to respond in the most practical way to those who provided it with the right fare, and other orchestras began to be formed, musical associations, local philharmonic

His Last Handel Festival

societies, and music-loving amateurs all began to give concerts and perform cantatas, oratorios, and what not. There was, obviously, less need for the fostering care of Manns when so many promising offspring had grown into vigorous being.

But although the life-labour of Manns was in some measure achieved, there was yet some work in store for the energetic old age of the great conductor. It is true that he was no longer obliged to do quite the immense amount of "collar-work" that had formerly been necessary, and thus was enabled to save his strength for his seventh and last Handel Festival, held as usual in June, of the year 1900.

A minor change may be mentioned, in regard to the days of the week on which it was held, which had always hitherto been Monday, Wednesday, and Friday. They were now altered to Tuesday, Thursday, and Saturday. An interesting fact is noted by the *Musical Times*, in the increase of lady-performers in the band from 8 in 1891 to 68 in 1900. Costa, adds the writer, would have none of them;

August Manns

Manns, ever gallant towards the fair sex, withdrew the ban. Of this 68, 51 were violins, 10 violas, 5 violoncellos, and 2 clarinets. The male altos, on the contrary, from being a force of 418 in 1859 had dwindled to 73 in 1900. The critics noted but few defects in the great body of singers, and Manns pursued his usual course upon the grand rehearsal day, of pulling up his forces and correcting them whenever necessary. Nor, be it remembered, was the conductor the only "Festival veteran" present, for Santley had reached his twelfth and Edward Lloyd his tenth Festival. Several novelties were found suitable for presentation, but it would take too long to mention these. At the close of the Festival Manns received a very remarkable demonstration of affection from the mighty concourse of performers and audience, and one can only conjecture how much greater that demonstration would have been had they known that it was the last time their venerated conductor was to lead them. Nearly all those critics who were present make mention of the youthful vigour and consummate skill which

Successor at the Palace

rendered it difficult to realize he was then in his seventy-sixth year.

During the year 1900 there was established at the Palace, chiefly through the initiative of the late Mr. Henry Gillman, the manager, an orchestra of amateur players, under the honoured conductorship of Manns. The writer well remembers the kindly but vigorous way in which he heard and disposed of the trembling amateurs who aspired to join the Society. It soon proved too much for his strength, however, and his friend and successor in the directorship of the Palace music, Mr. Walter Hedgcock, took up the bâton, which he has since held with much distinction to himself and advantage to the ladies and gentlemen of the Society which he directs.

In the autumn of 1900 Manns conducted two Saturday concerts with his old orchestra with all the old fire and *verve*, and in March and April 1901 there were five more orchestral concerts under his conductorship, the programmes of which contained many standard works. To this brief season belongs the episode related by Mr. Joseph Holbrooke in the following account of " My First

August Manns

Success," published in the popular journal, *P.T.O.*, of 30th November 1907:—

" While I was at the Academy I had composed ' The Raven,' and at the time I was on tour I was busy orchestrating it. While I was at Wisbech, where we played for two nights, I finished it. Remembering that my fellow-students at the Academy had often said to me, ' Why don't you try Sir August Manns?' I sent the manuscript to him. I certainly did not expect to hear soon from him; but, to my amazement, while I was still in the country there came a letter asking me to go and see him. I wrote and told him that I could not, as I was trying to earn my bread as a pianist in a wretched pantomime. Only a few days later an unexpected development caused me to go to London. In the company was another pianist, who was playing one of the parts. He thought he could make more money if he took on my job, so he managed to get the others to get rid of me. I told them I was perfectly willing to go if they would pay me the money that was due to me. After a fearful scene, they paid what they owed me, but gave me no railway ticket back to town. This I had to

Holbrooke's " The Raven "

borrow. As soon as I arrived, I went to Sir August Manns, telling him that I could go to the Palace. He made me stay to lunch with him—it was the best meal I had eaten for weeks—he said kind things about my music, even adding that he thought my troubles were over, as he meant to do 'The Raven' at one of the Saturday concerts. I pointed out to him that it was a project which could, unhappily, not be put into execution, for the simplest of reasons—I had no money to pay for the orchestral parts !

" My inability to pay was not allowed to stand in the way, for Sir August had all the parts copied at his own expense, instead of abandoning the production of the work, as I suggested. It was produced on a foggy November afternoon, under the conductorship of Sir August. I sat in front, in a world of amazement, listening to my own music, which I heard for the *first* time, if I exclude the attendance at the rehearsals. The effect it produced on me is indescribable. I defy the most bloated genius to describe his soul in torment or ecstasy ! I had never heard any of my orchestral works at the Royal Academy. At the conclusion of the performance the applause was very slight, but persistent, and it did not stop until I went on to bow, making, as one of the critics remarked, 'A raven-like spectacle in very *outré* clothes.' If that writer had only known the reason of this! I had no money to buy white collars, or pay for the washing of them, so I had to wear a muffler round my neck, and my shoes were very bad.'

The story of the few remaining years of Manns' life is soon told. Happily, they were full of peace and serene content. Not once or twice but often, and with the utmost simplicity and dignity, did the veteran speak or write of the approaching end of his fine career. Never was there the slightest hint of repining or discontent, rather were his closing years like that

" . . . Tide, as moving seems asleep,
　　Too full for sound or foam,
　When that which drew from out the boundless deep,
　　Turns again home."

Incidents similar to that mentioned by Mr. Holbrooke of Manns personally bearing the expense of copying orchestral parts were of common occurrence. It constantly happened, also, that

Failing Health

funds were not forthcoming to pay for extra band rehearsals, etc., necessary for a proper rendering of a work, and Manns never hesitated to spend his own money for such a purpose rather than have an indifferent performance.

In the beginning of 1903 it became evident that his health would hardly stand the strain of an eighth Handel Festival. This was the more manifest as it had become necessary to alter very largely the preliminary organization of the singers, a work entailing great personal labour and application to details. This part of the work Manns undertook to do if he were relieved of the other, and arrangements were made for Dr. Frederic Cowen to replace Manns at the conductor's desk. The directors of the Crystal Palace, however, by no means ignored or failed to appreciate the expert advice of their old and trusted servant, as the following letter shows:—

CRYSTAL PALACE,

July 10*th*, 1903.

DEAR SIR,

My directors at their meeting on the 8th inst, instructed me to write you to express in the heartiest

August Manns

manner possible their very high appreciation of your valuable assistance and the unflagging energy displayed by you during the recent Handel Festival. They consider that the marked success which has attended all the performances is due to your invaluable advice, and my Directors wish me to convey to you their sincere thanks for what you have done in conjunction with Dr. Cowen.

Yours faithfully,

J. H. COZENS,

Secretary and Acting Manager.

Immediately before the Festival, on the 12th May, Manns had been immensely gratified by the well-deserved compliment paid him by the University of Oxford in admitting him to the honorary degree of Doctor of Music. The following comment upon the event appeared in the *Oxford Magazine* of 13th May (see *Musical News*, 23rd May 1903):—

" The Honorary Doctorate of Music was yesterday conferred on Mr. August Manns, and certainly no recipient of that degree ever deserved it more. In his tenure, lasting over forty years, of the Directorship of Music at the Crystal Palace, Mr. Manns

Sir August Manns in his robes as
Doctor of Music of Oxford University.

Doctor of Music

carried on with unceasing enthusiasm a nobly artistic work, the influence of which on music in England is beyond all calculation. All these years daily concerts were given at which the entire literature of great orchestral music was played over and over again; and during the bulk of this time there was literally hardly any orchestral music worth mentioning to be heard in England outside Sydenham. The full band of the Saturday Concerts was famous throughout Europe. Mr. Manns first taught us to know Schubert and Schumann and many others, and, though a foreigner himself, had always the warmest welcome for British music. The star of the Crystal Palace began to wane when London concert-givers entered into the results of Mr. Manns' single-handed labours: and a new management with no love of art in its soul maimed, and finally dismissed, the superb band. Mr. Manns has never sought official distinctions, and honours which have been showered on musicians unworthy to be mentioned in the same breath have never come his way: and so we rejoice that, even though tardily, Oxford has done all that lay in its power to show its appreciation of a great life-work, which is one of the landmarks in the history of English art."

August Manns

The fitting sequel to this event took place at the final rehearsal of the Handel Festival Choir in Exeter Hall on 15th June 1903, when Dr. Manns was presented, on behalf of the choir, with academic robes and a beautiful silver bowl, weighing eighty ounces and of a sixteenth century design.

Mr. Frye, the choir superintendent, made the presentation, and spoke of the twenty years and the seven Festivals during which their conductor and chief had endeared himself to every one. He was then formally invested with the robes by Mrs. Manns, and a wreath of laurel that was sent anonymously was presented, with a graceful tribute, by Dr. Cowen. In reply, Manns made one of the touching little speeches he knew so well how to deliver, and the pretty ceremony came to an end.

The speech ran thus:—

" Ladies and Gentlemen, your warm-hearted reception gladdens my heart! It tells me that my efforts on behalf of the well-doing of musical art in England are appreciated, and that the honour

Cap and Gown

conferred on me by the Oxford University enjoys your sympathy.

" This evidence of my having gained the esteem —may I say the affection?—of those with whom I have had to do my musical work, constitutes a reward which I value very highly, and which fills my heart with gratitude for all who have helped me in winning the cherished prize.

" To you, Ladies and Gentlemen, I owe special thanks for the unceasing zeal and patient obedience with which you have always followed my musical leading during the many years we have made music together. Need I add that I feel equally grateful for the charming compliment you are paying me by presenting me with these luxurious academic robes.

" The possession of this handsome Musical Doctor's gown and this coquettish academic cap makes me feel proud and happy, because these pretty things will in future speak to me of my musical success and of that friendship and affection which have helped me in securing it.

" But, Ladies and Gentlemen, what can I say about the valuable additional present with which you have honoured me? How can I thank you adequately

August Manns

for it?   I can only assure you that I fully appreciate
the honour, and that I feel deeply grateful for your
generous and handsome gift—a gift which will show
in years to come that the Musical Director of the
Crystal Palace has had friends.

"Thanking you now once more very sincerely for
your unceasing kindness, I will only add that I hope
to regain in due time a fair measure of good health,
and be able to join you next spring once more as
your musical leader; feeling sure that in the meantime you will give Dr. Cowen's conductor's wishes
your very best attention, and thereby help him to
secure a grand artistic success at the approaching
Handel Festival; a success which will gladden the
hearts of all who love Handel's immortal music,
amongst whom you must place that old friend of
yours who has just been talking to you, and will
now bid you farewell, happily farewell, with a hearty
'Auf Wiedersehn.'"

In July 1903, the writer received a letter from
Manns dated from a hydropathic establishment
at Peebles, Scotland:—

"I am here since the 1st July to try the new
hygiene — namely, electric-heat   bath,   massage,

Knighted

mixed with a good deal of Father Kneipe's cold-
water, sun, and air treatment. I am glad to say
that my great enemy, rheumatism, is yielding, and
that I am now hopeful of regaining a fair measure of
good health, and be able to conduct a few more
concerts before joining the big band of King David
in the Unknown Land.

"Mrs. Manns, of course, is with me. We shall
leave on Wednesday next, the 5th of August, but
shall make a few excursions in the Highlands before
returning home."

Later in the year, on the King's birthday, the
entire musical world was deeply stirred with
pleasure by the announcement that the long-
looked for knighthood had been at length conferred upon Manns.

And now, indeed, a chorus of happy congratulations was poured upon the old musician. From
all sides came addresses, letters, newspaper
articles, complimentary cards, public dinners,
and personal kindnesses from the hosts of friends
who ever kept a warm place in their hearts
for August Manns. The pupils of the Royal
Normal College for the Blind, an institution in

August Manns

which he always took the keenest interest, serenaded him in his house in Harold Road, Upper Norwood. The staff of the Palace, his fellow-workers in the divine Art, Mr. Walter Hedgcock and Mr. Herbert Godfrey, the Musical Association at their annual dinner, and other representative bodies, gladly took the opportunity of placing upon public record their indebtedness to him.

From among the numerous letters received, space must be found for a few. Sir C. Villiers Stanford wrote from

50 HOLLAND STREET,
KENSINGTON, W.,
November 9th, 1903.

MY DEAR OLD FRIEND,

I am more than delighted at the announcement of the papers this morning. We all would have knighted you, or made you a peer years ago; but then you did not produce so many of the compositions of Cabinet Ministers as you did of the young Englishmen. Anyhow, we have never ceased to be grateful to you, and some of us in these latter days (who had happy experience

H. Gadsby and F. Corder

of your unbiassed catholicity of taste) to long for you and your influence again.

So long life to you, and every good wish from one of the musicians who has especial cause to be grateful to you.

Mr. Henry Gadsby, that most genial and kindly musician who passed to his rest but a few short months after his old friend Manns, wrote a similar letter, signing himself

"Ever yours truly and most grateful for so many kindnesses bestowed on me by you."

Frederic Corder, in an eloquent letter, wrote thus:—

My dear old Friend,

. . . When I remember—as how can I ever forget?—for how many years you were the sole champion and helper of the young English composers (my own success in life, for instance, is owing to nobody but you), how untiring you were in advancing the cause of orchestral music in England, with no reward to speak of but that of your conscience, with only a scanty meed of approval from the Press and a half support of the

August Manns

fickle public—when I remember all these things, I can only feel that all the knighthoods in the world would not express a quarter of what that world owes you. My own gratitude to you is too deep for words, and I gladly take this opportunity of letting you know how it burns within me, though I can never express it properly. May the rest of your life be as happy as those early years of unselfish labour must have been is the earnest prayer of one who is proud to call himself your friend and pupil.

Other letters, all warm-hearted and affectionate, came from many representative musicians, British and foreign—Elgar, Sir Hubert Parry, Sir Alexander Mackenzie, Joachim, William Wallace, Prout, Fritz Hartvigson, and many more.

Among the many congratulatory dinners to which Manns was invited was that of the Whitefriars Club on January 29th, 1904, when he delivered the following historical and retrospective speech in response to the toast of his health:—

With the Friars

"Worthy Prior, Friars, and Fellow-guests,—I thank you, Worthy Prior, most sincerely for the flattering terms in which you have referred to my musical work at the Crystal Palace; and you, Friars and fellow-guests, I thank equally heartily for the generous sympathy with which you have endorsed the Worthy Prior's courteous comments. Such cordial expressions of approval, and the many charming letters of congratulation which have reached me from all grades of society, verify the fact that my efforts on behalf of musical art in England have been understood and are appreciated, and that the honours conferred upon me last spring by the University of Oxford and quite recently by his Majesty the King enjoy very far-reaching sympathy.

"This result is particularly gratifying to me, because it testifies that my views about music for the people were correct, and that by judicious combating of the people's prejudices against so-called classical music by means of the programmes of my daily concerts at the Crystal Palace during nearly half a century, I have been able to make Crystal Palace music assert a decidedly beneficial influence upon the general development and healthy progress

August Manns

of musical art in England. London concerts, which
previous to Crystal Palace influence were all more
or less of a rather unsatisfactory, ' Hand-still ' type,
are now carried on on very liberal and refined art
principles, and a great many provincial towns are
steadily following suit. I will only mention one—
namely, Bournemouth, where Mr. Dan Godfrey, by,
as he says, working on the liberal lines of Crystal
Palace music, has actually lifted seaside music from
the streets into the concert-room, an achievement
which cannot fail to bear splendid fruit, and for
which he deserves the highest praise. Indeed, when
following the all-round music-making of to-day and
comparing it with that of fifty years ago, we can
rejoice in the fact that music has now entered the
national life of England more healthily than at
any previous period of its strangely chequered
career.

" Musical historians tell us that, according to a
tractate of the thirteenth century deposited in the
British Museum, 'music was lovingly patronized
already in the twelfth century at the Court of
Henry II., and that the Court singers, Magister
Johannes Felius Dei, and Macklebit of Winchester,
and Blakesmit and others, sang very beautifully.'

About Music

And it is generally known and acknowledged that England was pre-eminent in the cultivation of the Madrigal, which flourished from about the second half of the sixteenth till near the middle of the seventeenth century.

" These pleasant statements are strengthened by Shakespeare's and Milton's immortal lines about music. Shakespeare, in *The Merchant of Venice*, says grandly—

> ' The man that has no music in himself,
>   Nor is not moved with concord of sweet sounds,
>   Is fit for treasons, stratagems and spoils, . . .
>   Let no such man be trusted.'

And Milton, in his *Tractate on Education*, says—' Music, if wise men and prophets be not extremely out, has a great power over dispositions and manners, to smooth and make them gentle from rusty harshness and distempered passions.'

" Unhappily, this more than pleasing picture of the loving cultivation of music in England of the past is very rudely blurred by such ugly facts as the following:—John Locke, an Oxford savant, who was born in 1632, and who died in 1704, after having done appreciative work as a statesman,

August Manns

philosopher, and private tutor of the son and grandson of the great Chancellor of the reign of Charles II., the Earl of Shaftesbury, published, towards the end of the sixteenth century, a book called *Some Thoughts on Education*. In that book he (Locke) strongly disapproves of the cultivation of poetry and the companionship of poets, but goes much further with regard to music and musicians by saying—'I have among people of talent and men of business so very seldom heard a man praised or known to be esteemed on account of cleverness in music, that I feel justified in assigning to music the lowest place in the list of general accomplishments.'

"We are likewise told by Dr. Chrysander, in his *Biography of Handel*, that when in 1733 the Chancellor of the University of Oxford invited Handel to perform his oratorio of *Athalie* in connection with the University festivities of that year, a prominent Oxford man of learning, T. Hearn, said in his record of those festivities—'It was intended to have the Drama as well as Music represented at the Festival, but the Vice-Chancellor did not permit the actors to come to Oxford, and not without justice, although they might as well

Palace Concerts in 1855

have been here as *Handel with his beggarly crew of foreign fiddlers.*'

"From this strange record we are led to assume that John Locke's pedagogical principles of a couple of centuries ago have exercised a very evil influence upon the cultivation of musical art in England, an influence which was still at work fifty years ago. Indeed, Locke's dictum that 'it is ungentlemanly to cultivate music' was probably the root of that formerly often-heard ridiculous assertion, 'The English are not a musical nation.' Happily, that ridiculous assertion is now lastingly exploded, and is, to use a figure of Balfourian speech, 'as dead as mutton.' England has now a good many high-class schools of music, and is giving high-class musical training to thousands of young men and women of all grades of society.

"When I began my work in 1855 at the Crystal Palace, I could scarcely find half a dozen English composers whose works were suitable for the grand Crystal Palace Saturday Concerts. The catalogue of music performed at those concerts since 1855 contains the names of 343 composers, of whom no fewer than 103 were born and trained in England. First-class performances of choral and orchestral

August Manns

concerts are now successfully established throughout Great Britain. Of course these remarkable
improvements have naturally also raised the status
of the musician. The Chancellor of Oxford University in 1733 was severely blamed for allowing
'Handel and his beggarly crew of foreign fiddlers'
to take part in the great national festival of the
year; the present Vice-Chancellor is very much
praised for having conferred upon the conductor
of concerts for the people the much-prized degree
of Musical Doctor; and his Majesty the King has
honoured the same conductor by knighting him.
I feel deeply grateful for these distinctions, and
am happy in knowing that Crystal Palace music
has assisted me in gaining them."

The last occasion upon which Manns was seen
at the conductor's desk was that of the jubilee
of the Crystal Palace, when, upon the 11th June
1904, a commemoration concert took place, and
a presentation of a wreath was made to him.
Mendelssohn's " Hymn of Praise " was performed,
and many well-known singers, including Mr.
Santley, appeared.

The year 1906 was, it will be remembered, a

Ill-health

year of great heat, and the writer was told by Manns that he had found it very trying. Indeed, he was under the impression that his general ill-health dated from an occasion on which he had taken a nap upon a sofa one afternoon, with the sun shining full upon his face. But he seldom or never complained, save for a half-humorous grumble at his old enemy, rheumatism.

During the winter his weakness of health became more apparent and his appetite began to fail a little. He did not, however, let it interfere with his daily routine; he usually rose to breakfast, and in fine weather would take a little walk in the beautiful garden of the new home upon Beulah Hill—White Lodge—to which he had moved in the summer of 1906. Here he had the advantage of spacious grounds and wooded fields surrounding them, with a fine view stretching out to the Surrey hills in the distance. In the middle of February the writer called with a little daughter one Sunday afternoon, and although the veteran musician was not at all well, and was suffering from distressing weakness,

August Manns

yet he was fairly cheerful, took tea with his wife and guests, and even made a little jest. Immediately afterwards, however, during the ensuing week, he took to his bed, and upon March 1st, 1907, he died, aged eighty-two years all but eleven days.

CHAPTER VIII.

THE life-work of a great orchestral conductor
exercises an influence over that of his fellow-
musicians which is unique. A composer must
of necessity do his work alone, and he may
be pardoned for holding aloof from his fellows.
They are, in a sense, his rivals in art, and the
least selfish among frail humanity can hardly
claim total immunity from our common attributes. The public performer, vocal or instrumental, is bound to feel the sense of rivalry too
keenly within him to allow his better feelings
towards his fellows their full play. But a conductor is a sort of benevolent despot. He need
know no jealousy or rivalries; he remains the
arbiter of a musician's ambitions from the days
of his "pupillary" state up to the summit of his
artistic career. He is at once the friend and

August Manns

master of a composer, the patron of the public
performer, and the autocrat of orchestral artists.
If you add to all this the respect and demon-
strative affection of a mighty public, it is small
wonder, indeed, if the disease of "swelled head"
should sometimes become manifest. But from
this too common complaint August Manns was,
indeed, as singularly free as he was from all
narrowness of mind in matters musical.

Were it possible to include in this volume
letters from all the British musicians whom the
catholicity shown by Manns had enabled him to
befriend in the course of a long life it could not
be termed a memoir. It has already much out-
grown the proportions originally assigned to it.
But no apology is needed for the inclusion of
letters from representative men; rather is it
necessary to explain that of the many friends of
August Manns who would doubtless have gladly
sent reminiscences only a few could be asked
to do so. Among those is Sir Alexander
Mackenzie, Principal of the Royal Academy of
Music, the senior among the three great music
teaching centres of the kingdom.

Sir Alexander Mackenzie

Sir Alexander has kindly written the following
deeply interesting account of his early connection with Manns. At the same time he drew
attention to a letter written to the *Scotsman* newspaper shortly after Manns' death, which is here
reprinted, following his own communication :—

". . . It was in connection with Manns' visit
to Edinburgh with Wood's opera venture under
Anschütz as conductor that I first saw him. And
I can see the shock head of hair—only jet-black
then—now. My father being leader—or musical
director, as we would say now—was principal violin,
but alternated with Manns by personal arrangement, and this was the beginning of their friendship. I also remember being taken to the Crystal
Palace when I was about eight years old (and on
a visit with my father to London) to see Manns.
[This was about the year 1855, as Sir Alexander
was born in 1847.] My father died about a year
and a half afterwards, just after leaving me as
a boy in Germany. The first letter I ever got
announced his death.

"My own connection—professionally, I mean—
seems to have begun in 1878, or perhaps 1879,

August Manns

when I find that he played a Scherzo for orchestra (MS.) at the Crystal Palace, which had just been performed for the first time by Julius Tausch in Edinburgh or Glasgow. Manns followed him, I think, as conductor in Scotland; anyhow, I remember Manns urging me to write a Scottish Rhapsodie for the season, which I did, and my notes tell me that it was produced on January 5th, 1880, by Manns; and that was practically the beginning of my career as a composer. In 1881 he produced Scottish Rhapsodie No. 2, 'Burns,' on December 27th, in Edinburgh, also written for him. I only mention these facts to show how long back dates my acquaintance with him and how much I owed to him. Everything I wrote was always played without delay at the Crystal Palace, and we remained intimate to the last."

To the Editor of the " Scotsman."

March 4th, 1907.

Sir,—Referring to your interesting notice of the late Sir August Manns, I may mention that some years ago I purchased the pay-book of the old Theatre Royal, dating from 1853-55, in which his signature appears several times while he was a

Some Old Comrades

member of the orchestra connected with German
opera, organized by the late Mr. George Wood.
Thinking that it might be of interest to Sir A.
(then Mr.) Manns, I sent him one of the pages
containing his signature, and received a courteous
and characteristic letter from him in answer. The
letter, dated Crystal Palace, London, July 4th, 1900,
is in the following terms :—

" Let me thank you most sincerely for your kind
letter and interesting enclosure. I remember the
particulars of my engagement as a first violin of
the orchestra of Mr. George Wood's German-
Italian opera in Edinburgh and Glasgow at the
beginning of 1855 quite well. Of the names your
cutting of the pay-book contains those of Mackenzie,
Hausemann, Stehling, Stewart, and Brown remind
me of their owners very vividly. Stehling, the
principal viola, is still a member of my Crystal
Palace Saturday Orchestra, and was playing at the
last Handel Festival. The rest, alas! have all joined
the majority ; so, likewise, have the two conductors,
Anschütz and Orsini, and all the singers. Often
have my thoughts wandered back to those days of
hard work and little pay. I received in Edinburgh

August Manns

£3, and in Glasgow, where I took Mackenzie's place of leader, £4 per week. However, such hardships are a good schooling, and subsequent prosperity is enjoyed doubly by those who have known and suffered adversity. My connection with Scottish music, as conductor of the Glasgow and Edinburgh-Choral Union Concerts, was a reward for the honest struggles of my youth, which I thankfully and joyfully appreciated."

The Mackenzie mentioned was the father of Sir Alexander Mackenzie, the Stewart was Mr. R. B. Stewart, who died within recent years at an advanced age. At his benefit at the old Theatre Royal in 1827, the overture to *Oberon* was first played in Scotland.

It is interesting to note also that Sir August Manns conducted the Reid concerts of 1867-68.

Sir Charles Villiers Stanford, in a brief note regretting that he knew but little that was of public interest concerning Manns, recalls as a main point of interest for musicians, "his sturdy opposition to the von Bülow misreading of the Trio in the Scherzo of the Ninth Symphony, which Richter and later conductors adopt"

"Getting Old"

(vide *Internationale Musikzeitung*, Breitkopf and Härtel).

Only one member of the original Saturday Orchestra now survives. This is Mr. George J. Webb, elder brother of Mr. Samuel Webb, a well-known viola-player, and of Henry Webb, perhaps the greatest viola-player of the last half-century. Mr. George Webb, who is, we regret to say, in a feeble state of health, remembers the details of his early connection with the Palace while only a lad of sixteen years, very vividly. He joined the band under Schallehn, to play the E-flat clarinet, the very instrument Manns himself was engaged to play, and he left the orchestra in October 1897, after a period of 43 years and 5 months.

He informed the writer that the incident of the repetition of Sullivan's *Tempest* music on the following Saturday, which necessitated the cancelment of the programme as originally arranged, was unique in the whole of his long experience. And he related an anecdote of Manns replying to one of his orchestra named Reisland, who complained that he was getting old:—"No, no, you

August Manns

must not say that! It is a crime for a musician to be old." There is a pathetic significance underlying this that orchestral players will well understand.

Mr. Morel, a Saturday Concert player of later years at the Palace, remembers the kindness with which Manns treated the mother of one of his German players, who, speaking no English, had lost her way in the maze of streets near Sydenham. Guiding herself by the Palace building, she was at length brought to Manns, who, to her joy, spoke to her in her own tongue, found out her name, and put an end to her difficulties by placing her in a cab, which he paid for himself, and directing her to her son's address.

Professor Ebenezer Prout writes:—

" I never was on very intimate terms with Manns, and such personal intercourse as I had with him was mostly between 1870 and 1880, or, in general terms, some thirty or more years ago. So far as I can remember, I first made Manns' acquaintance in the early 'sixties. I was at that time one of the professors in the newly-opened Crystal Palace School of Art, and my engagements took me down to the

Professor Prout

Palace two or three days every week. With the active support and co-operation of Mr. (afterwards Sir) George Grove, then Secretary of the Palace, Manns was devoting all his energies to the development of the Saturday Concerts, which, thanks to him, obtained a reputation second to that of no concerts in Europe for the performance of the highest class of orchestral music. . . . During the time I was connected with the Palace I not only attended the Saturday Concerts regularly, but had also the *entrée* to the rehearsals; thus I had every opportunity of judging of his capabilities. No matter what the music to be given, whether it was sympathetic or not to him personally, he never 'scamped' his work. I do not believe that during the many years over which the concerts extended any piece was ever presented with insufficient rehearsal.

"The Crystal Palace Orchestra thus gained a reputation for highly finished performances, the credit of which was in no small degree due to the personal exertions of their conductor. The composers for whom Manns showed special preference were Schubert and Schumann. I well remember the excitement at Sydenham when Grove returned from

August Manns

Vienna (I think in 1867), bringing back with him the newly-discovered music to *Rosamunde*, which had been lost for nearly fifty years. His enthusiasm was fully shared by Manns, and few who were present at the first performance of the music will have forgotten the immense effect made by the two Entr'actes and the lovely Ballet-air in G minor. Schubert's great Symphony in C was a *cheval de bataille* with Manns. I have never heard such splendid performances of that work as under him. Hardly less fine was his reading of the unfinished Symphony in B minor, which he was the first to bring to a hearing in England. . . . English composers owe a deep debt of gratitude to Manns. At the date when the Saturday Concerts were commenced, a British prophet had emphatically no honour in his own country, and it was an extremely difficult matter for a native musician, to obtain a hearing at all. But Manns, German though he was, showed far more sympathy for rising English composers than, so far as I know, any English-born conductor has ever done."

When Dr. Campbell, the founder and Principal of the Royal Normal College for the Blind first

Dr. Campbell's College

came to London in 1871, he called on Sterndale
Bennett and explained his plan of locating a new
school (to introduce the American system of
training the blind) near the best musical centre.
Bennett exclaimed, "Well, then, go and see
Mr. Manns at the Crystal Palace." He also
gave him a letter of introduction both to
Manns and Grove. Upon finding Manns, Dr.
Campbell asked if his pupils could be allowed
free admittance to the concerts. He replied,
"Not only to all concerts, but to all rehearsals."
And after taking his visitor to Sir George Grove,
the matter was forthwith arranged. Manns took
the greatest practical interest in the new venture,
visiting the students frequently both at lessons
and at play, and becoming later, with Sir John
Stainer, one of the examiners to the College.
In 1877, he conducted, for the benefit of the
College, a grand evening concert under royal
patronage, at St. James' Hall, at which Joachim
played, supported by the Crystal Palace Saturday
Orchestra augmented to 119 performers.

Among Manns' many admirable characteristics,
one in particular stood prominent—his love of

punctuality; a legacy, no doubt, of his eight years' service under one of the greatest soldiers of modern times—von Roon. This extended not only over his professional duties, where, of course, it was of the greatest possible value, but into his home life, where meal-times and other fixtures were regulated with soldierly precision. The only " movable fixture " was his own hour for retiring to rest, which was of necessity governed by the occasional need for a late sitting to study a score. To do this he would stay up till three o'clock in the morning, reading, beating time, and making notes of the length of time occupied by various numbers.

There is little, if anything, more to be said of the career we have imperfectly endeavoured to trace in these pages. It is one that is singularly free from complexity, and it is therefore hoped that an unpretending account may not be un-welcome. Much has of necessity been omitted. It was not possible, for instance, to deal with the daily concerts that were, of course, as interesting in their way, almost as musically important, as the more ambitious weekly festival. Several

Pro-British Sympathies

other musical bodies, such as the Handel Society in 1894, were for a time under the direction of Manns, but it is believed that all the most important have been described.

It is not without interest to know that so fine a stock is not likely to soon die out, for besides a nephew in the English musical profession, the son of Mr. Otto Manns, a surviving and younger brother of Sir August, there are a brother and a sister still living in Germany, and a grandchild, Miss Louise Bönten, residing in England.

The vessels which ply across the narrow seas between our little island and the Continent have been aptly compared to the shuttles of the weaver's loom, which knit into a harmonious whole the varied races of the world. If this be so, as it most certainly is, how much more powerful a factor in the fusion of the races of mankind is such an one as August Manns, with his strong pro-British sympathies and his Anglo-German kindred, who must of necessity deplore any temporary cloud that darkens the mutual friendship of the two great countries that equally draw their hearts' best feelings from them.

APPENDIX.

(1) When Dr. Shinn was engaged in the preparation of his work on the Saturday Concerts, referred to elsewhere, he made a copy of the first programme of the series. This copy is here reproduced. It will be noticed that while the second part in each programme is identical, the first is entirely different. It is unfortunately now impossible to settle the point as to which is correct; for after a careful search at the Palace, the British Museum, the Royal College, and other likely places, the writer has been unable to find a copy of the original programme:—

CRYSTAL PALACE SATURDAY CONCERTS.

First Programme on Palace Books,

Saturday, October 20, 1855.

PART FIRST.

Coronation March   .   .   .   .   *Meyerbeer.*

Overture—" Martha " .   .   .   .   *Flotow.*

August Manns

Waltz—" Klänge vom Delaware " . . *Gungl.*

Finale—" Lucia di Lammermoor " . . *Donizetti.*

Quadrille—" Alliance " . . . *Manns.*

PART SECOND.

Overture—" Ruy Blas " . . . *Mendelssohn.*

Waltz—" Des Wanderers Lebewohl " . *Strauss*

Charivari . . . . . *Zuhlehner.*

Marien Redown . . . . *Manns.*

Overture—" Le Roi d'Yvetot " . . *Adam.*

AUGUST MANNS,

Musical Director.

(2) The following letter has an important bearing upon the situation at the time Costa's illness interfered with his duties. It is included by kind permission of Mr. Gordon Cleather, who was from September 1882 to May 1885 manager of the Crystal Palace :—

[*Copy.*] CRYSTAL PALACE,

May 8th, 1883.

DEAR MR. CLEATHER,

It has occurred to me, after due reflection, that I ought not to make *direct inquiries* about the

234

Appendix

conductorship of the Handel Festival conditional on Sir Michael Costa's failure through prolongation of his illness, but that I ought to entrust the matter to your care, inasmuch as you, as manager of the Crystal Palace Company, are the most responsible person in reference to the general arrangements. What, I think, you might do at the next Committee meeting is to point out that Sir Michael Costa's precarious condition of health seems to make it necessary that some other conductor should be requested to prepare himself for conducting the rehearsals and performances in case of Sir Michael's failure, and that I, as the Musical Director of the Crystal Palace Company, ought to be honoured with such a request, inasmuch as I have already gained my spurs in connection with the Handel Festival Choir, through my having had to conduct the rehearsals and performances of Mendelssohn's *Œdipus in Colonos* and Mr. Sullivan's Prince of Wales' Te Deum, and having also had to perform conductor's duties for all the rehearsals and general preparations of the Rossini Festival, and have, moreover, presided as conductor over at least half-a-dozen grand choral displays at the Crystal Palace, in connection with the Sultan's, the Russian Emperor's, and other festivities with honourable results.

Assuring you, and every one else who may care about it, that I wish from my whole heart that Sir Michael Costa may be able to take his old place, I beg to say, on the other hand, that I do not in the least fear the great responsibility which would fall to my share in the next Handel Festival should I have to conduct it even if I should have to do, as it would be, only " deputy duty," and accommodate myself to Sir Michael's general arrangements.

The United Kingdom does not contain a musician who knows the acoustic properties of the Crystal Palace as well as I do, and who has had as much experience in conducting large festivals than,

Dear Mr. Cleather,

Yours faithfully,

A. M.

P.S.—Please keep this away from the eyes of other officials, etc. It is a delicate matter and easily capable of misconstruction and misrepresentation.

(3) By the courtesy of Sir Hubert Parry and Mr. F. Pownall the writer is enabled to include

Appendix

the four highly interesting and characteristic letters written by Manns after witnessing some of the performances by students of the Royal College of Music:—

[*Copy.*] CRYSTAL PALACE, S.E.,

December 11*th*, 1902.

MY DEAR SIR HUBERT,

My heart has prompted me ever since the performance of *Fidelio* to write and tell you and Stanford how gratifying it was for me to witness the glorious result of the sound and careful training of the students of the Royal College of Music on that occasion. The doings in the orchestra as well as on the stage evidenced high artistic guidance throughout the whole of the performance, and Stanford deserves special thanks for his judgment and care as conductor.

I, having in the earlier years of my musical career played in turn the second flute, second violin, and first violin at performances of *Fidelio*, and conducted several concert performances of the opera at the Crystal Palace Saturday Concerts,

August Manns

know the various difficulties of Beethoven's score
intimately, and was therefore all the more delighted
with the artistic re-production by your students.
Were the horns played by pupils of the R.C.M.,
and who was the first? Their charmingly discreet
and " safe " playing deserves the highest praise.

All your principals deserve credit for the con-
scientious study of their respective parts. Most of
them have, to the best of my judgment, a fair
chance for gaining prominent positions on the
lyric stage if they continue their musical art studies
in trust of the wisdom and truth of the following
little poem, called

THE FOUR " P'S.

Patience, Perseverance,
Prudence and Pluck,
They who practise these shall always have luck;
Those who neglect them,
Whatever they be,
Shall never succeed on land or on sea."

Please present my compliments (the compliments
of an old brother-musician) to all your young
hopefuls, and ask them (particularly your beautiful-

Appendix

voiced young Leonore) to read in Grove's *Musical Dictionary* the article on "Madame Schroeder Devrient's Life and Art Career." It will tell them how she—the greatest of all Fidelios—achieved greatness. I saw her (and heard her) Fidelio in Danzig about fifty-seven years ago, and fell helplessly in love with her.

Here ends my letter.

What do you and Stanford say to Weber's *Euryanthe* for your next students' opera? It has four splendid principal parts and some very fine choruses.

With kindest regards,

Yours sincerely,

(*Signed*)   AUGUST MANNS.

[*Copy.*]   "GLEADALE," HAROLD ROAD,

NORWOOD, S.E.,

January 15*th*, 1905.

MY DEAR SIR HUBERT,

Many thanks for your kind letter. Unhappily, something has gone wrong with my *musical*

August Manns

ear. When trying a piano at Bechstein's about six weeks ago, which I wished to present to my daughter, I discovered that certain notes were distressingly sharp.

The first four or five sounded about a semi-tone, *and the rest a full major second higher than struck.* The doctors have since tried to solve and heal this phenomenal ailment, but without success; and their final verdict is that the bones connected with the ear-drum are hardened, and that advanced years (the chief cause of the trouble) stand in the way of an easy cure. Now, although spring and summer warmth will probably assist the doctors in their efforts to put my ears *in tune* once more, it will be best that you do without me at your next examinations. Please do not communicate these particulars to more of my friends at the College than you can help. I still hope to conduct one or two more concerts, and a general talk about my present disturbed *musical* hearing would prejudice any further conductor's efforts.

Please convey my hearty greetings to my young friends, your young *College hopefuls,* and tell them that their highly meritable, artistic reproduction of Gluck's *Alceste* has given me great pleasure, and

Appendix

has strengthened my belief in their future well-doing as carefully-educated artistes.

With kindest regards,

I am, dear Sir Hubert,

Yours sincerely,

(*Signed*)   AUGUST MANNS.

[*Copy.*]   "GLEADALE," HAROLD ROAD,

NORWOOD ROAD,

March 30*th*, 1905.

DEAR MR. POWNALL,

I have by this post written to Miss Tout and thanked her for posting me the words of the pieces selected for the 13th April. Will you kindly assist our young friend in finding the words and send same by an early post?

Richard the Second tried my poor old musical head yesterday rather severely; indeed, the most radical of radical composers demands too much of poor mortals. Even your clever young students were yesterday a good deal adversely affected by the terrible effort to bring sunlight into a musical forest which has too many big trees overgrown

August Manns

with formless creepers. They (your youngsters) did not do so well as formerly in their *trial at sight-reading*.

With kind regards,

Yours sincerely,

(*Signed*) AUGUST MANNS.

[*Copy.*] " GLEADALE," HAROLD ROAD,

NORWOOD, S.E.,

April 5th, 1906.

DEAR MR. POWNALL,

. . . With regard to my exhaustion after the examination, no doubt the interest in Richard Strauss' strenuous music with its display of " *the extremes of musical modernity*," as I have described it in my report, had something to do with it. Such music requires a new system for the study of harmony for musicians who acquired their theoretical knowledge and formed their musical taste, like my poor self, more than sixty years ago. Musical ears trained through *pre-Richard Straussian music* only are seriously harassed by the unceasing crushing dissonant-chords, disconnected tonalities

Appendix

and diffusive counterpoint. I cannot find impressive beauty in such music, hence my exertion when listening to it. But by that I do not mean to say that Stanford did wrong by bringing it before his college pupils. On the contrary, such musical liberalism of a professor of a musical college is deserving the highest praise and has my fullest appreciation. My report, which you will receive by this post, will tell you more about my personal views on this important point.

Hoping that Parry and Stanford will be pleased with my report.

I am, as always,

Yours very sincerely,

(*Signed*)   AUGUST MANNS.

(4) In a catalogue of compositions performed at the Saturday Concerts the following appear under the name of "A. Manns":—

Violin Concerto in E. First played (by himself) 8th December 1855, and several times in later years.

August Manns

Idyll—"Farewell to Switzerland." First played (by himself) 1st December 1855.

Serenade for Violoncello. First played 10th November 1855.

Paraphrase for 'Cello and Orchestra on Härtel's "Abend-ständcher." Played 21st April 1888.

Festival Overture. Played 14th March 1863.

ERRATA.

Page 4, line 13, *for* "No. 9" *read* "No. 8."
,, 46, ,, 12, ,, "nine" ,, "eight."
,, 166, ,, 4, ,, "Grove's letter" *read* "Mr. Bennett."
,, 230, ,, 22, ,, "as interesting in their way" *read* "as interesting and in their way."

THE WALTER SCOTT PUBLISHING CO., LTD., FELLING-ON-TYNE.

For EU product safety concerns, contact us at Calle de José Abascal, 56–1°, 28003 Madrid, Spain or eugpsr@cambridge.org.

www.ingramcontent.com/pod-product-compliance
Ingram Content Group UK Ltd.
Pitfield, Milton Keynes, MK11 3LW, UK
UKHW040616240426
470322UK00010B/163